THE LANGUAGE LIBRARY

DICTIONARIES:
BRITISH AND AMERICAN

THE LANGUAGE LIBRARY

EDITED BY ERIC PARTRIDGE
AND SIMEON POTTER

ALREADY PUBLISHED

JAMES ROOT HULBERT

DICTIONARIES:
BRITISH AND AMERICAN

ANDRE DEUTSCH

TO MY DISTANT FRIEND
ERIC PARTRIDGE
WHO GAVE ME THE COURAGE
TO WRITE THIS BOOK

CONTENTS

DICTIONARIES: BRITISH AND AMERICAN

No reference book, perhaps no book of any kind except the *Bible*, is so widely used as 'the dictionary'. In Anglo-Saxon countries even homes that have few books or none at all besides 'the Scriptures' possess at least one volume of the sort. Business offices are likely to have dictionaries; and most stenographers have a copy on their desks. At one time or another most girls and boys are required by their schools to obtain and use dictionaries. And English dictionaries can be purchased almost anywhere – in drug stores, the news stands at railway stations, even some supermarkets, as well as news dealers' shops and book stores. Some people carry a vest pocket dictionary constantly on their persons.

To be sure, the use of such reference books is often merely to determine the correct spelling of words, or to find out the accepted pronunciation of words. Such functions of dictionaries cannot be regarded as intellectually important perhaps, but they do have social importance: for the person concerned it is a matter of moment that he does not suggest to others by misspelling a word in a letter or memorandum or by mispronouncing it in talk, that he has not been well educated or is not 'well-bred'. Perhaps it should be added that dictionaries are in demand as helps in solving crossword puzzles; in fact I have seen in pharmacies and five-and-ten-cent stores volumes whose dust jackets proclaimed that they were designed expressly for use in working at such puzzles – I wonder how honestly.

Despite this common experience with dictionaries, the average person is likely to have many erroneous ideas of them and little understanding of how to interpret them rightly, in fact how to use them profitably. Thus it is often thought that the mere presence of a word in a dictionary is evidence that it is in accepted use. Though most if not all such books have a system of characterising words as obsolete or in slang use, and marking as slang or colloquial certain meanings, many people, especially if their use of the word which they are looking up has been challenged, are likely to conclude that if they find it in their dictionary it is in reputable use.

Curiously enough, in holding such views people could cite good authority, but it would be that of a hundred years or so ago. The aim of dictionaries for a long time after the beginning of the eighteenth century was to exhibit only what was in the best use, the words, spellings and meanings employed by the best authors, and all else was suppressed; indeed it was not uncommon for the lexicographer to assert emphatically that no 'low' words would be found in his book. Evidently that practice so impressed the popular mind that it is still not conscious of the great change which has taken place in the preparation of present-day dictionaries. Such a cultural lag is by no means rare: elementary text-books and books on scholarly subjects prepared by 'popular' writers for the general public frequently express ideas or state as facts hypotheses which scholars in the subject have not held for fifty years or more; for instance, it is still asserted that Chaucer was born in 1328, though real authorities on his life have long held that his birth date was about 1340, or more recently 1343 or 44; and the story that Shakespeare as a boy held horses for gallants during performances at the theatre is still retailed, though there is no evidence for it.

Similarly the non-bookish layman almost invariably supposes that one dictionary is as good, as authoritative, as another. In the United States this misapprehension is strengthened by the fact that any publisher may ascribe his book to 'Webster', a potent name not only because of its historical eminence in lexicography and the fact that the excellence of some of the books which bear it has given it prestige, but because 'the man in the street' is convinced that it is that of the great orator and politician, Daniel Webster, whose powerful personality has made a strong impression on the folk mind, as witness the story 'The Devil and Daniel Webster'.

Finally there is a false notion that 'the dictionary' has

absolute authority. Its statements are used frequently to clinch arguments; in part this idea derives from an entirely proper use of a dictionary by lawyers or judge in court, or by a pastor in a sermon, when the purpose is merely expository, to make clear the meaning of a passage; in such cases a dictionary definition has a certain advantage because it cannot have been coloured in any way by the speaker, but only rarely can particular circumstances make it valid as part of the proof, and then only if all dictionaries agree substantially (otherwise the opponent can invalidate the 'proof' by citing another dictionary). There is of course an exception to this generalisation, namely, when agreement has been made in advance that the statement of a particular dictionary shall constitute final proof. Otherwise the authority of dictionaries is only that of the men who made them; naturally, however carefully they proceed, they are fallible; and it is easy to show that reputable dictionaries often disagree in their judgments; indeed, a new edition of a dictionary may reverse the stand taken in a preceding issue; for example, there are great differences between the 1909 edition of the *Merriam-Webster* and the 1961 edition in the hyphenation of compound words.

It would be possible to make general statements like those in the preceding paragraphs about all the respects in which popular conceptions of the dictionary are wrong. But either they would not be convincing to a thoughtful mind or they would have to be taken on the authority of the person who made them without understanding of the facts which warrant such sweeping statements. So a more detailed explanation of the essential facts should be given; and it is hoped that many of the facts will be interesting in themselves.

DICTIONARIES IN GENERAL

The dominant sense of the word *dictionary* for English-speaking people is a book which presents in alphabetic order the words of our language, with information as to their spelling, pronunciation, meaning and (as something more or less unintelligible and pointless) their etymology. But of course that is only one type of dictionary. There are dictionaries of more limited scope, as of medical terms, slang, dialects, and there are dictionaries of all the well-known languages on the globe, in particular bi-lingual lexicons such as Greek-English, Latin-German, etc. By what we think of as an extension, due to the fact that dictionaries are reference books with entries arranged in alphabetic order, the word is applied to books which do not deal with words: for example, there are 'dictionaries' of history, the social sciences, biography, especially the great *Dictionary of National Biography* and its more recent American counterpart.

At a fairly early period in the cultural growth of many civilised peoples, a need has been felt for a dictionary or glossary of their languages; so there are ancient Greek, Sanskrit, Chinese and Celtic dictionaries; and in the case of less highly cultivated nations, modern specialists in their languages have produced such works. In my copy of the *Encyclopædia Britannica*, the eleventh edition, there is an impressive bibliography of dictionaries classified according to languages. About a few of them interesting details are given briefly. Of one author, named Castellus, who in 1669 published a two-volume dictionary of 'Hebrew, Syriac, Samaritan, Aethiopic and Arabic in one alphabet; Persian separately', we learn that it 'occupied him for seventeen years, during which he worked sixteen to eighteen hours a day'. Edward Lane, familiar to us as the translator of *The Arabian Nights* which we read in our childhood, spent seven years in Cairo working on an Arabic dictionary; he used as his basis a native lexicon in twenty-four 'thick quarto' volumes; finally, I add only one more item, as the reader may not be so intrigued about this sort of thing as I am: we are told that an English translation of one native Chinese dictionary would fill one hundred and forty volumes octavo of one thousand pages each. Details as to how such enormous length was achieved are not given.

THE ORIGIN OF ENGLISH DICTIONARIES

In what follows it will hardly be necessary to return to the work of lexicographers in other languages, for the origin and development of English dictionary-making has been but little affected by the lexicography of other countries; authors have proceeded as though there were no compiling of such books elsewhere. Of course this statement does not mean that English lexicographers have not known about the existence of dictionaries on the Continent; from 1650 onward Englishmen mentioned the dictionary of the Accademia della Crusca in Italy and the lexicographical activities of the French Academy; and Samuel Johnson mentioned explicitly the dictionaries of those academies; naturally the makers of *The Oxford English Dictionary* and all contemporary lexicographers know of what is done elsewhere; but it is difficult to perceive any considerable influence of these foreign works on English dictionary-making.

The steps in the development of English lexicography are quite clear, and the whole process curiously parallels the doctrine of evolution which affected thinking so much in the nineteenth century. Once the idea that all biological species, no matter how highly developed and specialised, derived by more or less minute gradations from quite simple organisms – the theory of evolution – had become widely accepted, it was applied by a sort of analogy to non-biological phenomena, especially to human institutions and man's arts. So studies of this, that and the other activity or achievement of mankind were published not merely to exhibit the growth or development of the subject, but to suggest that the development was a *natural* one like that of a biological species. Perhaps as long as one does not think that there is a force which compels the development of social institutions and practices by minute gradations, there is no harm in the application of the word *evolution* to social phenomena. Such usage however has caused an extension of the meaning of the word so that now there is ambiguity in the use of it; hence when Sir James Murray, the editor of *The Oxford English Dictionary*, delivered a lecture, later published as a pamphlet, entitled 'The Evolution of English Lexicography', it may be that he meant merely the history of English dictionary-making. But he would have been justified for intending something close to the more rigid meaning of the word *evolution*, for the history of English dictionaries, like that of the early English drama, shows a curious similarity to evolution in the biological sciences. To be sure there is, as in the case of the drama, one large break in the sequence, a new step not specifically prepared for by what went before; but that too might be paralleled by the biological phenomenon which the Dutch scientist de Vries called *mutation*.

Let us see just what happened. English dictionary-making began in Anglo-Saxon times, that is before the Norman conquest, and it grew from a practice which in itself had nothing to do with dictionaries. This was the habit of glossing manuscripts of Latin writings such as the gospels and the psalter. In the study of languages in school today and perhaps always, many students unwilling to spend the effort required to memorise the meanings of the words in the assigned texts, after looking up the words in their glossaries or dictionaries, write the English equivalents between the lines and just above the foreign language words. In so doing they are making glosses like those in many medieval manuscripts.

In Anglo-Saxon times, however, it was not always a lazy school boy who glossed a text. Sometimes the work was consciously planned and carried out so systematically that the result is an interlinear translation of the original. The most beautiful manuscript of our Anglo-Saxon period, the Lindisfarne Gospels, the text of which was Latin, when naming those who participated in the making of the volume, includes the glosser, who was one Aldred; and the Rushworth manuscript of the gospels states that it was glossed by the owner, a priest named Farman, and by a second person named Owun. Presumably such glosses were made for the use of readers who did not know Latin: in Lindisfarne the members of the convent; in Rushworth perhaps persons to whom Farman might want to lend the book, though one would suppose that there were few laymen who could read even English. It may be that Farman's hold on Latin was weak and that he got at least some of his meanings from friends or some Latin dictionary; the fact that the English that he used was that of his district, however, suggests that he was but little influenced by books.

Occasionally such glosses were used by studious men in the Anglo-Saxon period as a means of increasing their Latin vocabulary. For such a purpose a man would abstract the words from the volume and make a list of them with their English equivalents. To this list he might add other glosses from other books. We have such simple and complex lists, with sometimes explicit indication of the texts from which they were taken. In other cases when no titles are given, it is possible to identify the sources from the correspondence of the list with the order of words as they appear in the books concerned.

Finally the process of alphabetisation of the complex lists began. First all words beginning with A, all those whose initial was B, C, etc., were separated out and put in blocks together without regard to the second letters of the words. Then alphabetisation of the first two letters appears. Finally alphabetisation was carried out throughout as in a modern glossary. So by the end of the Middle English period Latin-English lexicons were in use, and in the sixteenth century French-English dictionaries were made on the same principles. Moreover, by 1450 English-Latin dictionaries were being made; indeed, three of the best-known early dictionaries are of this type: the *Promptorium Parvulorum*, the *Catholicon Anglicum* and (1570) *Manipulus Vocabulorum*. Evidently the boys of those days had to do Latin prose, as those of my generation did.

The makers of the simple glossaries, the lists of collected glosses and the dictionaries into which the glosses developed, would have been astonished if they had been able to foresee the use to which their work would be put in our day, namely, as evidence of many early English words not found in the books which have survived to us from those times, of the form of others not found till considerably later than the glosses, and of the sounds and grammatical forms used in the dialects of Anglo-Saxon.

Thus far the chain of development is unbroken, and it has led to the production of ordinary, and generally brief, bilingual dictionaries. To make the Latin-English, English-Latin and corresponding French dictionaries of our day requires only a wider range of vocabulary, improvement in definitions and other refinements. But dictionaries which explained English words by English equivalents could not derive directly from the bilingual ones; a new start had to be made. There is a similar situation in the history of the English drama; its development was an evolution up to the appearance of the morality play. For that there is no regular link with what had preceded; someone with an original mind had to think of the possibility of applying the current dramatic method to allegory. Much the same sort of thing happened in dictionary-making.

THE FIRST ENGLISH DICTIONARIES

Apparently until the sixteenth century no one felt any need for a book which would give English definitions of English words. Then in 1582, an English schoolmaster of a remarkably original mind, Richard Mulcaster, suggested that it would be useful to have a dictionary containing all the words in the English language, showing their correct spelling and meaning. No such 'English-English' dictionary, however, appeared for nearly forty years. When the first such book was published it was meant to satisfy an unusual need; this was to make understandable to the general public the many words appearing in English books but not used in ordinary speech.

There were two chief reasons for the introduction of such words in English writing. The first was to enable authors to express ideas for which there were no native words. Even in Anglo-Saxon times writers had been faced with the necessity of increasing the vocabulary of English so that they might convey the ideas and information which they found in the Latin books which they were translating or adapting into English, especially words of philosophic and theological import. At first they tried to gain this effect by compounding English elements; for example, they wrote 'learning-boy' for Latin *discipulus*; or they used a loose equivalent such as 'younger one' for the same sense. But well before the end of the Anglo-Saxon period the practice of simply transferring the words from the Latin books into the English translations and sermons came into vogue. This practice became dominant, and in the whole later history of English the users of it have never hesitated to introduce into their writing and later into their speech words for which they thought they had need from any language on earth. It may be interesting to contrast the custom of German in this respect, for German has resisted as much as possible the tendency to adapt words from foreign sources and has followed the practice which, we have seen, was in use in early Old English; thus instead of 'immortal', which is from Latin, the German says *unsterblich*, which is equivalent to un-die-able, though -able itself is Latin. In later times the practice of adapting elements from Latin or Greek was extended so as to provide technical terms for scientific use and new inventions, e.g. *appendicitis, bronchitis, telegraph*. Even in such cases German tries, not too successfully, to get along with native compounds; thus one dictionary gives for 'bronchitis', *Luftröhrenentzündung*, but for 'bronchial cold' it has *Bronchial-katarrh*; for 'telephone' it has *Fernsprecher*, i.e. distant-speaker, but for 'telegraph' it offers only *Telegraph*.

In addition to the need for expressing in English meanings for which the language did not have words, a second motive for the introduction of foreign words appeared as early as the fifteenth century in the verse of Lydgate; it was the desire to attain expression in an elegant and ornamented style; in simpler terms, to 'dress up' the English language. Many writers during the fifteenth and sixteenth centuries followed Lydgate's lead by importing large numbers of words from French and Latin; in their belief they were 'enriching' the English language, which in itself was too poor and crude for effective use in artistic writing. The ornate diction of Sir Philip Sidney's *Arcadia* affords hundreds of examples of this 'aureate' style; and the books of more learned sort like Sir Thomas Elyot's *Governour* used hundreds of other intellectual words borrowed from French or Latin. It is perhaps of interest to note that although many of these words had no continuing life in English, like *beauperlaunce* (fine language) and *hodiern* (belonging to today), others are in ordinary use, e.g. *abridgement, satisfactory*. There was objection to this practice, of course, some 'purists' holding that any enrichment should be derived from the native stock of the mother tongue; hence arose that attempt to revive obsolete words and to make compounds from the older stems which is familiar to us in Spenser's vocabulary. Many of these words

B

were quite as strange to the general reader as the ornate terms from Latin and French.

How was the ordinary reader, of little or no classical learning and no acquaintance with Middle English literature, to comprehend the meaning of the authors who used such terms? It must have been quite impossible for him to do so; in some cases perhaps he could get the general sense of a passage even though he 'skipped' the strange words, as many a youngster of our day does, but in more instances he must have been baffled. Such writing was for an upper class, as Sidney's and Lodge's novels were, or for scholars, as Gabriel Harvey's books were. By 1604, however, the first effort to resolve the dilemma of the ordinary reader was made by a schoolmaster named Robert Cawdrey. The title of his little book is telling: *A Table Alphabeticall, containing and teaching the true writing and understanding of hard usuall English words, borrowed from the Hebrew, Greeke, Latine, or French, &c.* This little volume of only 120 pages was followed by others, each longer and including more words than its predecessor, and the fact that some of them went through several editions is indication that they satisfied a need. It is amusing to note that the title page of Cawdrey's book and those of some of its followers state that they were prepared with the needs of gentlewomen in mind. Perhaps then, as now, women were more avid readers than men; but as little effort was made to educate women in Latin and even French, they were not so well equipped for comprehending the borrowed 'hard words' as were men who had had grammar (i.e. Latin) school and university training and who therefore could supply the meaning of the Latin word in the passage in which the borrowed expression appeared.

Though mention is made on Cawdrey's title page of 'the true writing', i.e. the spelling of these words, their real reason for being was to give the meaning of the 'hard words'. This was always the primary purpose of these books, but as early as 1623 a second aim, characteristic of its time and of the attitude toward English style, appeared. This is found in a book by Henry Cockeram which was divided into three parts, the first explaining the hard words, the second giving the elegant

equivalents of 'vulgar' words, and the third devoted to mytho-
logy. The purpose of the second part was to enable anyone who
used it to transmute plain, simple writing into stately and ornate
language. In general these small volumes provided information
as to spelling and meaning but none of the other features which
we expect in a dictionary now. None the less these books did
lead up to the publication of the first English dictionary which
aimed to include all the words of the language.

EARLY COMPLETE DICTIONARIES

This was the *Universal Etymological English Dictionary* of Nathaniel
Bailey, the first edition of which appeared in 1721. As the title
indicates, Bailey's interest was largely in the etymology of
English words, and as that interest would apply quite as much
to simple, homely words as to learned ones, it was perhaps the
determining motive for extending the entries to include the
entire vocabulary of English. This book was issued in twenty-
four editions by 1782, and it continued to be reprinted till 1802.
It is said that a copy of the edition of Bailey which appeared in
1731 was the basis which Samuel Johnson used in compiling his
dictionary; this edition was the first such book which paid
attention to pronunciation; as in Johnson's work it indicated
the place of accent in polysyllabic words.

Partly no doubt because of the influence of dictionaries like
Bailey's, but more because of cultural influences, by mid-
eighteenth century a greater consciousness of the importance of
'correct' English had developed than had ever existed in
England. Early modern writers had felt and expressed dis-
satisfaction with English as a medium for literature, as compared
with what seemed to them the perfection which they appreciated in the style of classical Latin literature. They were
apologetic and disparaging in their references to their employment of the mother tongue in writings meant to have dignity
and artistic refinement. Some of them actually composed
books in Latin as More did his *Utopia*; others like Ascham
said that it would have been easier for them to do so. Now
by the middle of the eighteenth century the attitude had
changed.

Respected authors like Dryden, Pope and Addison, not even considering the possibility of using Latin, had devoted themselves to English with such good effect that there seemed to be a chance that English might attain the standard of classical form and style; people now were proud of the achievements of writers who had used their native language, and there was much discussion of methods of 'purifying' English and then 'fixing' it, that is, stabilising it so that it would remain unchanging in the perfection that would be attained. Men like Swift were much concerned about the 'corruptions' which appeared in the writings even of eminent authors and about the 'licentiousness' in the use of English which had developed in the preceding period. When one examines the discussions of this subject one is struck by the triviality of the 'corruptions', e.g. the use of the first syllables only of longer expressions, such as *mob* for *mobile vulgus*, *incog* for *incognito*, the omission of *e* in weak pasts, e.g. *drudg'd*, *rebuk'd* (though of course these had been in use as far back as Shakespeare's time), and neologisms, some of which are now in unquestioned usage, others long dead. It is true now of some older people that they dislike *photo* and *auto*, but we do not excite ourselves about such popular uses. In the eighteenth century they insisted that the language must be purged of such 'corruptions'.

Except in the Anglo-Saxon period English culture had always lagged behind that of the Continent. So it is not surprising that these ideas of purifying the language had made their appearance in Italy and France as early as the late sixteenth century, that 'academies' were founded for the purpose of purifying the language, and that by the seventeenth century these had produced dictionaries. Cultivated Englishmen were acquainted with the activities of the Académie Française and the Italian Accademia della Crusca, which were devoted to the purification of French and Italian; and there was much discussion in favour of the founding of an English academy for the purpose of fixing and improving the English language. Some writers opposed such an academy, among them Samuel Johnson, who thought that his dictionary could perform the function of correcting English better than an academy could. Actually the reverence felt for his dictionary, the authority that it shortly acquired, did cause it to have great influence on the linguistic usages of English people for a long time.

People were willing to devote considerable labour to the effort to acquire a mastery of English comparable to that of their respected authors. So books on grammar were published to establish correct syntax and the proper forms of words, and finally Samuel Johnson's famous dictionary provided the standard by which correctness in spelling and the meanings of words could be determined. Though Johnson realised, as statements in his preface indicate, that it is the nature of language to grow and change, he did consciously attempt to regulate and improve English and to discourage the use of words or meanings which seemed to him to be barbarous. To some extent this effort to legislate for the language is to be found in most later dictionaries, but as time goes on lexicographers try more and more to record merely what they find to be true in the use of words.

At the time that Johnson began work on his dictionary, he was not the distinguished literary personality that he later became; indeed he was hardly more than a Grub Street hack. The idea of making a new dictionary was in fact not his but that of a group of booksellers who employed him to make it. The prestige which in course of time came to be attached to his dictionary was in part due to its notable qualities, but also in part to the commanding position which he attained in the world of letters. Indeed no other English lexicographer has had anything approaching Johnson's standing as author and literary panjandrum. While he was engaged on the *Dictionary* Johnson wrote and published his series of periodical essays, *The Rambler*, which added greatly to his reputation. The dictionary, when at last it appeared, was at once successful, and for seventy-five years, in one form or another, it was the unquestioned standard of usage.

The chief innovation of Johnson's dictionary was its illustration of the meanings of words by quotations from the writings of well-known authors; though Johnson was the first to use such quotations in a dictionary of English, he did not originate the practice, which was familiar to him in dictionaries of the classics, the dictionary of the Accademia della Crusca, and Richelet's French dictionary. The effect of this practice was not only to confirm and make clear the meanings of the words as Johnson defined them, but to show how the best authors, the men whose style and form was most highly regarded, had used them. The information that we have of his method of obtaining these quotations is that he read the books which he wished excerpted, marking the words which he wanted to illustrate, and that his six assistants copied the sentences in which they occurred on slips of paper, just as a modern reader for a dictionary does. Presumably these were then alphabetised and so made available for use as examples. Johnson gave few specific references, however, for his quotations, often citing the authors only; because of the vagueness of such references it was possible for him when he needed a quotation to produce one from his memory, and it has been surmised that he often did this.

Not much more of Johnson's method of work can be discerned. One biographer says: 'An interleaved copy of Bailey's dictionary in folio, he made the repository of the several articles'. If so – and some use of Bailey is certain – what he entered on the blank leaves and the revisions of Bailey's text which he may have made on the printed pages must have been only a skeleton of the 'articles' rather than the complete articles, for Bailey's book would hardly have provided the space necessary for Johnson's much longer copy.

Revisions of Johnson's dictionary appeared after his death for more than a century. The latest I have seen is one published in 1866 by R. G. Latham, formerly professor in University College, University of London, on the basis of Henry Todd's revision of Johnson. This work, in four stout volumes, adds quotations of later date than Johnson's time. It seems strange that such a book could be thought of value as late as its date of publication; it adds no further guidance on pronunciation to Johnson's indication of stresses.

Johnson's failure to give guidance as to pronunciation (aside from marking the position of stress) was due not to lack of interest or consciousness of the importance of the matter, but to his realisation of the wide variety of English pronunciation, especially in the local dialects, the speakers of one dialect being at times unintelligible to those of another, and his consequent disbelief in the possibility of fixing a standard. In addition there were hosts of words whose pronunciation differed greatly from what would have been expected from their spelling. In truth the speech of a cultivated English man or woman of the eighteenth century would sound provincial, even rude to us. For example, *er* plus a consonant was pronounced generally *ar*, as it still is in the British pronunciation of *clerk* and the general pronunciation of *sergeant*; thus *marchant, sarvant*. Similarly the ending *-ure* was commonly sounded *-er*, thus *nater* for *nature* and *figger* for *figure*. The ending *-ing* was pronounced *-in* by well-bred people, and words like *boil* and *join* were *bile* and *jine*. Indeed something like that divergence of spelling and pronunciation noticeable in some well-known surnames such as *Taillefer* (Tolliver) and *Beauchamp* (Beecham) was common enough in many words in ordinary usage. These were chiefly instances in which pronunciation had changed since spelling had become fixed. One of my favourite fictional detectives, Sir Henry Merrivale, in the most recent of his adventures that I have read, says: 'I came of a generation who said "ain't" and "don't" and "gal" and the rest of it as naturally as we said huntin' and shootin' and fishin' '.

The process which has turned back the pronunciation of English to patterns which had been entirely abandoned is a curious phenomenon in cultural history and perhaps the most remarkable evidence of the potential influence of lexicography.

The eighteenth century interest in ascertaining and fixing English usage extended naturally to pronunciation. As we have seen, Johnson did not attempt to prescribe pronunciation, but in two ways he did provide the basis for the regularisation of it; one was by uttering a famous dictum that 'those are the most elegant speakers who deviate least from the written language'. What history may lie behind Johnson's idea I do not know; at any rate his authority was no doubt all important. Of course the conception was as wrong as it could be: in the development of language, spelling is secondary, a more or less rough and ready attempt to record speech, and in English since the Middle

Ages it has been at first a mere welter of variants and then an unsystematic rigidity full of inconsistencies and anomalies. Johnson's other contribution to the establishment of a standard pronunciation was providing authoritative spellings which in the main proved satisfactory to the English-speaking world.

Now that Johnson had established standards of meaning, spelling and usage of vocabulary, people began to turn their attention to correct pronunciation, and interest in it was aroused by several writers and lecturers. Most prominent of these public exponents of elegant pronunciation were Thomas Sheridan, father of the dramatist, and John Walker, both of whom had established reputations as lecturers and teachers of pronunciation. Both had been actors, and so their conception of desirable pronunciation was bound to be the somewhat artificial uses of the stage and of oratory. After the publication of several pronouncing dictionaries by Scottish and English authors, there appeared in 1780 Sheridan's and in 1791 Walker's dictionaries. For a time there was some warfare between the supporters of the two books; this was resolved eventually in Walker's favour (though revisions of Sheridan appeared as late as 1811) apparently because of the argument that since Sheridan was an Irishman he could not be so authoritative an arbiter of *English* as Walker was.

No doubt Sheridan and Walker did in the main record the actual pronunciation of cultivated people of their time. But in all those features indicated above, such as the pronunciation of the ending -*ing*, and in many uncertain accentuations and sounds, they applied an artificial standard, that of spelling. In this they were guided largely by what they named 'the principle of analogy', which amounted to this: if a certain group of letters is pronounced generally in one way, it should be pronounced so in any isolated or disputed cases. [This meaning is not in *The Oxford English Dictionary*, probably because the word occurs in the first part published. Naturally there are more oversights in the first parts than in the later volumes.] Boswell records an instance in which Johnson applied this principle; he pronounced *heard* with the same vowel as that in *hear* because 'if it were pronounced *herd*, there would be a single exception from the

English pronunciation of the syllable *ear*, and he thought it better not to have that exception'.

Walker's method may be illustrated by his consideration of whether *obdurate* should be stressed on the first or the second syllable. He writes: [We] 'derive the adjective *obdurate* from the Latin participial adjective *obduratus*; and no analogy can be more uniform than that of removing the accent two syllables higher than in the original: thus *desperate, profligate*. . . . Agreeably, therefore, to every analogy of derivation, *obdurate* ought to have the accent on the first syllable.'

The vogue of Walker's dictionary was as great as that of Johnson's. In course of time appeared publications which inserted Walker's pronunciations into Johnson's text. Joseph Worcester prepared an edition of this sort: an abridgement of Todd's Johnson with Walker's pronunciations inserted in the entries. The number of editions of these dictionaries – Johnson's alone, Walker's alone (a revised edition of it appeared as late as 1904), and the two in combination – testifies to the great public interest in 'correct English', which had in the minds of many the importance of being evidence of good breeding and good social standing. It is amusing to note that in 1764 John Wesley published a dictionary whose title page emphasises 'hard words which are found in the best English writers', and has this: 'N.B. The author assures you, he thinks this is the best English dictionary in the world.'

NOAH WEBSTER

The next notable step in the development of English dictionaries was made in the United States by a man almost as remarkable as Johnson, though his productions, aside from his speller and his dictionary, were ephemeral. Born in 1758, Noah Webster had had a full life before he turned to the making of dictionaries. An early, brief experience as school teacher convinced him of the need for improvement in the text-books for English. So he published a grammar, reader and speller. The last had such wide acceptance that, as has been stated often, the income from it was sufficient to support him and his family for the rest of his life. In addition he engaged in politics, published arguments in favour of adoption of the Constitution of the United States, and wrote many books. In 1806 he made a trial flight in lexicography with the publication of a small dictionary. Immediately thereafter he started work on his large dictionary, which appeared in two volumes in 1828 under the title, *An American Dictionary of the English Language*. He lived to complete a revision of this, which he had to finance and publish himself, and which came from the press in 1839–41, when he was already in his eighties.

Webster was a man of original, even iconoclastic ideas, which he advanced in the uncompromising manner characteristic of some men who are sure that their ideas are right. In particular he had the temerity to criticise Johnson's dictionary vehemently in print. Even in the revisions that had been made of Johnson since his own day, Webster saw much that did not agree with American usage – like the later Mr Mencken, Webster was a stalwart American – and the definitions seemed to him cumbersome and sometimes, for ordinary readers at any rate, unintelligible. Perhaps if Webster had been less pugnacious in manner, his animadversions against Johnson might not have aroused the disfavour they did. Today at least it is to be hoped that informed people would realise that any book, any work of human hand and brain, is imperfect. That is the reason revisions of books, notably dictionaries, and new biographies of famous people, new surveys of history, etc., are published. To be sure, even now statements are made frequently in print to the effect that so and so has produced the 'definitive' treatment of this subject or that, as if no further discoveries about it, no new ideas concerning it, would ever come into being. Fortunately thought and knowledge never stand still. Of course Johnson's dictionary has faults, and so has every other dictionary of English or of any other subject that has been published. The violence of Webster's strictures on Johnson, however, was due only in part to lack of tact; he saw that Johnson's enormous prestige was checking progress and making it impossible for him to get the support he needed in order to bring out a vastly better book.

The effect of these attacks on Johnson, of the publicity matter concerning his dictionary which he sent out, and of his activity in promoting the sale of his books – he used to travel about, interviewing school-boards and urging them to 'adopt' his speller – was to arouse antagonism, from which he suffered all the rest of his life. Who was this cantankerous egotist, his detractors said, who thinks he knows better than the great Johnson? Even after the publication of his large dictionary and a rather wide recognition of its merits, Webster had to meet opposition in the form of competition from a book 'hastily shovelled together', as his friends said, by a former associate of his, Joseph Worcester.

As has been said, Webster had an original mind; in his lexicography he showed his vigorous independence in improving or correcting Johnson's etymologies, in attempting to reform spelling, and in recognising the pronunciation actually current in New England. Many conservative people objected to his effort to simplify spelling and to his stress of American usage, which they felt had the effect of driving a wedge between English and American culture. It was such people who supported Worcester in the 'War of the Dictionaries', which began before Webster's death and continued for twenty years thereafter. Amusingly enough there was also a regional element in the choosing of sides, Webster receiving support from Connecticut and his Alma Mater Yale, and Worcester from Massachusetts and Harvard.

Information about Webster's methods of work unhappily is lacking. His copy of Johnson, which is extant, is heavily annotated with expressions of disagreement with Johnson's statements and additions to the information given there, but it is merely a working copy and does not give anything like the entries which are in his own book. The only other certain knowledge we have is that the entire manuscript of the dictionary is in his handwriting. It seems improbable, however, that he worked entirely without assistants. At least we know that Alfred Percival read proofs of his 1828 dictionary. Evidently at one time Webster had some relation with Worcester, though later that gentleman became his chief competitor, for a year after the appearance of the dictionary, an abridgement of it made for Webster by

Worcester was published. Possibly Worcester assisted Webster on the large dictionary; possibly some of the members of his family helped him; at any rate, after his death, his son-in-law, who was professor at Yale, edited the third edition of the book. During Webster's stay in France and England while he was completing his dictionary he was accompanied by his son, then in his middle twenties, who later was one of the chief collaborators on the third edition and whose name appears on the title page of abbreviated editions from 1846 to 1867. In addition there were six other children from twenty to thirty-eight years old at the time the dictionary was published. Experience of academic life, and in particular of the way in which scholars draw on their wives and students for assistance in preparing their books, makes it seem most likely that the lexicographer, who was in his late sixties, did not actually do all the work himself; Webster was a great individualist and perhaps the sort of man who is unwilling to acknowledge the assistance of collaborators.

At any rate, in spite of personal unpopularity and the competition of Worcester, Webster's dictionary had a great success, replacing Johnson's in American use and being widely used in England perhaps chiefly because of the simplicity and clarity of the definitions and the addition to the vocabulary of many words which were in usage but had not previously been admitted by other lexicographers.

FROM WEBSTER TO THE PRESENT

As we have seen, Webster himself made a revision of his work, which was published shortly before his death. After that event two brothers, George and Charles Merriam, who were established as printers and booksellers in Springfield, Massachusetts, secured the rights to Webster's dictionary from his family and initiated two policies unique in the history of English dictionaries – that of limiting themselves to the publication of dictionaries, and that of bringing out a thorough-going revision of their main book and its abridgements at moderate intervals of time. The first of these revisions, which as we have seen was edited by Webster's son-in-law, appeared in 1847, and was bound in one volume. Thus the practice which has generally been followed to this day by commercial dictionaries of presenting the entire work no matter how enormous between one set of boards was inaugurated. This first single volume form of 'Webster's' comprised 1,452 pages; the latest edition has 2,662 pages.

Unfortunately when the Merriams obtained the rights to Webster's dictionary they were unable to secure the sole right to the use of Noah Webster's name. I say unfortunately because, as a result, the name *Webster* on a dictionary is now misleading. It purports to mean something distinctive, people purchase a *Webster's* dictionary supposing that it is authoritative; but actually it may be one of the best or one of the worst dictionaries that can be found. That name may be attached by anyone to a dictionary, and numbers of publishers more interested in profits than in actual contributions to lexicography have taken the opportunity to issue dictionaries called 'Webster's'. Sometimes the books so printed are earlier editions of the Merriam series on which copyright has lapsed; sometimes they are basically such editions which have been revised or augmented to some extent; sometimes they are said to be entirely new works. Books of this character can be bought almost anywhere, in five-and-ten-cent stores, in pharmacies, newspaper shops, even in some supermarkets; in an advertisement of the eighteen-nineties the Merriams stated that the books which were being sold then were cheaply-made reprints of an old edition and that they were on sale at dry goods stores and groceries. These volumes are, I believe, always of the abridged type; usually their price is little enough; and they may meet the needs of many who purchase them. Certainly they show the correct spelling, give some indication of the meaning of the words, and provide a passable pronunciation; but anyone contemplating the purchase of a dictionary should realise that they have no authority whatever and are often far from up to date. The company which succeeded the original Merriam brothers has done what it could to make the public understand the character of these books by publishing advertisements explaining the facts, by coupling the name *Merriam* with that of

Webster in their publicity, and by taking legal action against publishers who laid themselves open to such action. For some time, I understand, other publishers who used the name *Webster* had to state in advertisement and title pages that the volume was not put out by the publishers of the original *Webster* dictionaries. But even that safeguard, whose significance probably would be comprehended by few buyers, is no longer required legally.

The practice of coupling Webster's name to a dictionary which has no real connection with him continues, and sometimes in connection with a book that is being extensively advertised. For instance, in the *New York Times Book Review* of March 22, 1953, appeared a two-page advertisement of *Webster's New World Dictionary of the American Language, College Edition.* This stated that the book 'is *not* a revision of another dictionary'; the only justification that it makes for use of the name Webster's is this: 'a staff of trained lexicographers, linguists, editors and associates, counselled by specialists in the arts and sciences labored long and patiently, building on the broad foundations laid down by Noah Webster'. Just what this last expression means, I do not know. That it is based on one of old Noah's dictionaries? That it simply used the lexicographic methods that Webster and also all other dictionary-makers used? Then there are comparisons with two other desk dictionaries, asserting that this one contains 142,000 entries to the 125,000 entries of one and 132,000 of the other, and 1,760 pages to their 1,232 and 1,472. Advertisements for this book have appeared in *The New Yorker* and, of all places in the world, *PMLA*, the journal of the Modern Language Association of America. Obviously this is an ambitious effort; a pity that it could not stand on its own merits, whatever they are. A friend of mine who has used it tells me that its etymologies are the best to be found in any medium-sized dictionary.

Another instance of the meaningless use of 'Webster's' appeared in an advertisement in the *New York Times Book Review* of November 22, 1953. This announced the publication of *Webster's Unified Dictionary and Encyclopedia*, which was said to contain 1,700 pages and sold for $14.95. The advertisement makes no statement of the reason for using Webster's name and does not name any editor.

To return to the original *Webster's* dictionaries, a reprint of the 1847 edition, with additions, is the first illustrated dictionary published in America. The story is told that the Merriams learned that Worcester's third edition, soon to appear, would be illustrated. As it was impossible to insert pictures in the text without resetting the entire book, hastily procured cuts were put together as a supplement of eighty-one pages; for each picture there was a reference to the place in the text where the name of the object illustrated was inserted. The supplement was so popular that even after, in later editions, the pictures were in their proper places, the publishers did not dare to omit it; and so it appeared even in the latest *Merriam-Webster* published in 1961. One can only guess that, in a time when few books or magazines had illustrations, these pictures entertained the children whose parents had purchased a *Webster's*.

Webster's chief rival, Joseph E. Worcester, must have been a prodigious worker. Consider: in 1828 appeared an edition made by him of an abbreviation of Todd's revision of Johnson, with Walker's pronunciations inserted in their proper places and all Johnson's and Walker's preliminary matter (how much labour this book required I do not know; it may have been based on some British abbreviation with the pronunciations already included); in 1829 his abridgement of Webster's 1828 was published; and in 1830 a dictionary of his own on a smaller scale than Webster's 1828 came out. In 1846 this was followed by a large dictionary and this in 1850 by an abridgement. Worcester continued active, producing revised editions of his dictionaries until his death. Even after that, as late as 1881, a reprint of his large dictionary was published, and in 1920 a reprint of one of the shorter forms of it appeared. It is said his publishers contemplated a revision but desisted because of the great expense involved.

To conservative, cultivated people of the time, Worcester's books seemed preferable to Webster's because of their closer approximation to British standards, their use of what seemed a more refined type of pronunciation, that of the educated speakers of cities like Boston, in contrast to Webster's more rural pronunciations, and their preference for established usage in spelling. Something perhaps of the difference between Worcester's work and Webster's can be discerned by a glance at a surviving portrait of Worcester, which shows a pleasant, gentle, scholarly gentleman, a marked contrast to the assertive, not to say combative appearance of Noah Webster.

Worcester's dictionaries, though excellent of their sort, made no real advance in lexicography. If Webster's personality had not aroused so much animosity, it is likely that Worcester would have remained a compiler of text-books on geography and history and a remaker of other men's productions and would never have been encouraged to make a book of his own. More important in the evolution of English lexicography is the next work to be considered here – *The Century Dictionary*. To make clear the character of the *Century*, I must go back to 1850, when an Englishman, John Ogilvie, published the *Imperial Dictionary*, 'on the basis of Webster's dictionary' as the title page says. At a time when revisions of Johnson were still being published and American dictionaries were being offered to the British public, a new British dictionary, perhaps especially one which called itself 'technological and scientific', was naturally welcome. To be sure another Englishman, Charles Richardson, had in 1836–37 published his really remarkable dictionary, distinguished by its wealth of quotations, but, though frequently reprinted, it had made no general impression on the public, perhaps because it did not seem as practical, as useful, as Webster. It is significant of lexicographical conditions that in 1850 Ogilvie, an Englishman, should base his work on Webster rather than Johnson. At any rate, his book was successful, was revised from time to time and appeared in abridgements, some by Charles Annandale. Even as late as 1913 a revised form of it appeared in New York. In 1883 Charles Annandale published an enlarged edition of *Ogilvie* as an encyclopedic dictionary. Prior to that, publication of another encyclopedic dictionary had begun; because it was issued by various publishers it has been referred to by several names, such as *Cassell's Encyclopedic Dictionary*, *Lloyd's*, etc. In seven volumes, this appeared between

1879 and 1888; and it had considerable vogue in England, though not, as far as I know, in the United States. The inspiration for making this book was probably derived from the great French work of Larousse. The second English book of this kind, Annandale's revision of *Ogilvie*, in four stout quarto volumes, was successful.

The term *encyclopedic dictionary* defines itself; it is a work which combines the elements of encyclopedia and dictionary. Like a dictionary it aims to treat the entire vocabulary of the language, providing definitions and possibly pronunciation and etymology. Like an encyclopedia it gives explanations of the things named, including even historical information, but it does so more concisely than a full-scale encyclopedia does.

Annandale's *Ogilvie* was so well liked that the Century Company, one of the most prominent publishing houses of the period in America, reprinted it in the United States. A few years later the president of the company conceived the idea of making an American encyclopedic dictionary of similar scope. He obtained the right to use as much of *Ogilvie* as seemed desirable and engaged a staff of specialists, headed by Professor William D. Whitney of Yale, a world-renowned scholar of general linguistics and Sanskrit. Since the first parts of the resulting book (1889–91) appeared after the publication of the first parts of the *Oxford Dictionary* in 1884, it was possible for the editors of the *Century* to get ideas of method and form from that work, but it owed more to Annandale's *Ogilvie*. In addition to giving encyclopedic information, notably on scientific and technical subjects, the *Century* provided copious quotations and exceptionally exact and clear definitions. Some years later the original work was followed by a supplement, which in later printings was incorporated in the binding of the volumes of the main work by being added at the back of the volumes. This was an admirable book and, as no other work has replaced it, it is still valuable for reference purposes. It is unfortunate that the *Century* has never been revised as the Webster dictionaries have been. The nearest approach to a revision of it appeared in 1927: *The New Century Dictionary*, based on matter from the *Century* with additional material, in two volumes. This last, I

C

have been told, is still sold extensively by subscription and, combining as it does encyclopedic with dictionary features, it may be an excellent 'buy' for rural households.

For a number of years *Merriam-Webster's* chief competition came from Funk and Wagnall's *Standard Dictionary*. First published in two volumes in 1893–94, this work in later years has been bound in one volume. The aim of the publishers was to make this *par excellence* a practical dictionary. Its editor was the head of the publishing house which had undertaken the work, Isaac Funk, who had been trained for the Lutheran ministry and had the degree of Doctor of Divinity. As far as I have been able to find out, he had had no experience in lexicography, but he had ideas as to what was desirable in a modern dictionary and the ability to arouse respect, loyalty, and even affection in the staff which he organised. It was an achievement for such a man with an entirely green staff to turn out such a dictionary as the *Standard*, even with the customary collaboration of experts. Probably Dr Funk's experience as a publisher stood him in good stead, and no doubt he had a nucleus of able young assistants who, with a minimum of experience, could operate efficiently in dictionary work. One of these, the genial Frank Vizetelly, who succeeded him in the editorship of the *Standard*, became in course of time a sort of arbiter of usage for the American public, being interviewed by the press on neologisms, idioms, etc., and writing letters to the newspapers and short articles for magazines. Funk was responsible for putting the etymologies at the end of the entries and limiting them to a minimum of space; probably he was responsible also for the pictures, including colour plates, unusual at that time. The book was so well liked that it was adopted as a standard of 'style' in many printing houses and newspaper offices. Its abbreviated forms also had wide sale and use. The later history of the book is not easy to trace; apparently it has had only one revision (in 1913), but sufficient change is made in the course of reprinting to warrant the conferring of copyright at frequent intervals. The resulting effect is odd: I have seen an 'edition' dated 1945 which lists at the beginning the specialists who collaborated in the work, actually the specialists who were engaged on the original publication, men who died about the time that I was in college.

Undoubtedly it is less costly to make continual revision in successive printings than to prepare a completely new edition; and it has some advantage to the user in making available without delay corrections and additions that ought to be made. At any rate, I judge that makers of encyclopedias and similar reference books are finding such continual revision more feasible than the production of entirely new editions. But there is an obvious practical disadvantage in that if one quotes a book under continual revision, the owner of a different copy of the book may not be able to verify the quotation or check its context.

With the possible exception of the *Century*, all of these dictionaries and others not named (for example, in the United States, *Winston's* and *The American College Dictionary*, in England Wyld's *Universal Dictionary*) have been intended for general use, and all of them have been essentially commercial projects.

ABRIDGED DICTIONARIES

The two American works just cited are not so extensive as the complete *Merriam-Webster* or the *Standard* or *Century* dictionaries, though *The American College Dictionary* runs to 1,432 pages. It is true that the popular demand is for a moderate-sized book, both because such a dictionary is much cheaper and because it is handier for use in office, school or even home, where it can be kept on a shelf or with other objects on a small table. Nearly all of the inexpensive dictionaries, whether new compilations or reprints of early *Websters*, are of this size. To meet this demand it has long been customary for publishers to issue small books of this sort, sometimes more or less independent compilations, sometimes abridgements of larger standard dictionaries, such as Johnson's. The earliest abridged dictionary prepared by the author of the basic work was John Kersey's *Dictionarium Anglo-Britannicum*, 1708, which was based on his *New World of Words*, 1706, itself a revision of Edward Phillips's *New World of English Words*, 1658. Johnson published an abridgement of his dictionary, and Webster produced one of his 1806 book. Even before that an item in a New Haven newspaper of 1800 states that the publication of small dictionaries for schools was part of his plan. Though Webster's first abridgement (1807) did not sell well, that of 1817 did better. Finally after the publication of his two-volume book in 1828, Worcester, as we have seen, prepared for Webster a condensed version of that work. No doubt Webster anticipated a larger sale for the abbreviated book than for the original; and his expectations were realised, for the book sold well, supplementing the somewhat meagre income from the speller, and it was reprinted regularly for more than twenty years. Webster's practice has been imitated by publishers to the present time, so that it is possible to buy a *Merriam-Webster* in several sizes down to a little paper-backed volume in the series called *Pocket Books* for twenty-five or thirty-five cents. Similarly there are shortened forms of the *Standard Dictionary* and even of *The Oxford English Dictionary*. This last has been put forth in two chief forms, of which the briefer is much the better known. Though *The Oxford English Dictionary* was not completed till 1928, *The Concise Oxford English Dictionary* appeared for the first time in 1911. The title page and preface stress the fact that the *Concise Oxford* is not, as the work on which it is based definitely is, a historical dictionary, but is one of current usage. This book, in my copy, which is dated 1931, comprising 1,444 pages, had a wide acceptance, even in the United States, partly no doubt on its own merits as a usable book, but maybe chiefly because it was felt that it had the authority of the best British use and of the great work on which it is based. A still shorter form of the *Oxford* has been put out as *The Pocket Oxford Dictionary*. After the success of the *Concise Oxford* a larger abridgement appeared under the title of *The Shorter Oxford English Dictionary*. This has a narrower appeal as it is historical; it attempts to give a digest of the etymological information of the original and to trace the developments in meaning, and it reprints key quotations.

The other method of building a short dictionary is, necessarily, the one used by all 'ethical' competitors of the abbreviated books just mentioned: the compilation of an entirely independent work. That this is no small undertaking is shown by the fact that

The American College Dictionary required the co-operation of 355 experts and advisers. Books of not so wide a range as that one, however, have not needed so large a staff. Perhaps mention should be made of the *Thorndike-Century Dictionaries* which were prepared specifically for use by students in the grades and in secondary schools. These books had their origin in the ideas and research of Professor E. L. Thorndike, a well-known authority on education at Columbia University. The chief idea was that the words and meanings included should be only those which school children of particular grades would be likely to hear or to encounter in reading. What these words and meanings were to be was determined by count of the words in actual reading matter of different types. The details of the word count seem to a plain man like a philologist's fantasy – 270 assistants examining and classifying the words found in reading-matter comprising 4,500,000 words. The words so selected as being in wide usage, with some additions of recent date and some technical words which it was realised users of the dictionaries might meet, were then defined in terms which it was thought would be understood by the classes of people for whom the books were designed. For aid in defining and illustrating these dictionaries the publishers secured the right to use whatever the editors thought desirable in *The Century Dictionary*. Proponents for dictionaries made in this fashion contend that they are better adapted to the users for whom they are intended than dictionaries 'cut down' from larger ones, for the definitions in the latter were formed for mature readers, those in the former for children. What the truth is I can't pretend to know; only teachers who have used both types of books with classes are in a position to make a sound, impartial judgment. The feeling that the *Concise Oxford* or Merriam-Webster's *Collegiate* possesses an advantage in being based on the work of notable scholars working over a period of many years may be a fallacy, even though an elderly student of English may cling obstinately to it.

The *Thorndike-Century* books, *The American College Dictionary* and a still more recent publication, *The Thorndike-Barnhart Dictionary*, 1951, were prepared under the general editorship of Mr Clarence Barnhart; and the Thorndike word count was used in the two books intended for the general public as well as in the school texts.

A NEW KIND OF DICTIONARY: 'THE OXFORD ENGLISH DICTIONARY'

Let us return to the main line of our thought, which comes now to the magnificent *Oxford English Dictionary*. The purpose of the *Oxford Dictionary* (long called the *New English Dictionary* and still referred to by many under that name or by the abbreviation *N.E.D.*) was quite unlike that of any other English dictionary; it was in fact to trace what might be called the biographies of the words in our language, to show when they were introduced into our speech, if they were not found in the oldest stage of the language (variously called Anglo-Saxon or Old English); to show the development of each meaning and its historical relation to the other meanings of the word; and in case of words or meanings which have become obsolete, the date of the latest occurrence which could be found. All this was done by means of dated quotations, usually single sentences containing the words. Another new feature was the display of spellings in separate blocks by centuries, so that one can see at a glance the spellings which prevailed in each century since the first appearance of the word in English. In addition, the *Oxford Dictionary* included the other information customarily provided in modern dictionaries, indication of accepted spellings by means of the spelling of the entries, pronunciation, and etymologies (the last much more full and detailed than in other dictionaries). The work, whose first part was separated from the last by forty-four years, or if the *Supplement* is taken into consideration, by forty-nine years, and which required more than seventy-five years of labour from the first collection of material to the completion, is surely one of the greatest achievements of the human intellect.

As far as is generally known, the conception of *The Oxford English Dictionary* occurred not in the mind of one man but in the discussions of the (London) Philological Society. But a sentence in the Historical Introduction to the corrected re-issue (p. vii) of 1933 reveals that the father of the conception was Frederick James Furnivall, who for more than fifty years was one of the most distinguished and certainly the most dynamic among English philologists. His magnificent white beard and moustache, and his startling bright eyes made him in his later years one of the most picturesque figures in London. His great, indeed indispensable service to the *Oxford Dictionary*, in addition to conceiving the basic idea of it, was not in editing, though he was the second titular editor, but in securing by means of his Early English Text Society the publication of hundreds of Middle English (and some Old English) texts which till then were hidden in manuscripts, and thus making them available for dictionary use. Without these publications it would have been impossible for the *Oxford Dictionary* to give any proper presentation of the early history of thousands of English words.

According to this *Introduction*: 'That a forward step (in the development of English dictionary-making) was made . . . was due to the action taken by the Philological Society in the summer of 1857, apparently as the result of a suggestion made by F. J. Furnivall to Dean Trench in May.' What followed is well known and has been told often. Richard Trench, at the time Dean of Westminster but later Archbishop of Dublin, had published two small books (*The Study of Words*, 1851, and *English Past and Present*, 1855), perhaps the earliest of a long line of popular expositions of the fascinating history of our language and of selected English words. These books may not have had worthy competitors for a long time; at any rate, fifty years later when I was haunting second-hand book shops, I used frequently to see them upon the shelves; and in later time they have been republished in Everyman's Library. Prompted by Furnivall then, Dean Trench read before the Society a paper 'On Some Deficiencies in our English Dictionaries', which was published shortly. This paper brought to definite expression the main desiderata which the *Oxford Dictionary* was to satisfy. At once the Philological Society set to work to gather the material, at first for a supplement to the best existing dictionaries, later for a new complete work. Volunteers offered to help in the collection of this material by reading books and extracting quotations which it seemed might be useful. In 1859 Herbert Coleridge, great-nephew of the poet, was appointed editor. Coleridge was very active in laying plans for the dictionary and in supervising the gathering of material, but unfortunately he died in 1861. Furnivall was his successor in the editorship, but perhaps because he was not suited by temperament for this kind of work or, more likely, because of his absorption in promoting the Early English Text Society and the other publishing societies that he founded, there is no indication that he devoted much time to editing. He did, however, contribute thousands of quotations, jotting down sentences from his daily reading, even of newspapers.

Meanwhile the quotations continued to accumulate. A committee of the Society had prepared a list of books to be read, assigned the books to volunteers and sent them the standard slips on which the quotations were to be written. In themselves the slips were not unusual: in the upper left-hand corner the word for which the quotation was taken was written by the reader, the sentence containing the word was copied and a page reference was noted; in some cases the name of author, title of book and date of publication were written by the reader below the quotation; in others those facts were supplied by a rubber stamp after the slips were received by the editor, or were printed on the slips before they were sent to the reader. The amount of material obtained in this way in no great number of years was prodigious; in 1879, we are told, it totalled a ton and three-quarters. By 1881 the number of readers was 800, some of whom had sent in as many as 11,000 slips. In 1884 the editor reported that one reader had sent in 100,000 quotations, and another 36,000. It is improbable that any such co-operation from unpaid readers could be obtained now; certainly we had nothing like it when material was being gathered for the *Dictionary of American English*. People are 'too busy', actually too much engaged in making their way in a hard world, to have the leisure to extract quotations for a work which will not contribute to their fame or prestige. But in that quieter world before the first World War there was an educated leisure class, hundreds of cultivated men, living on inherited wealth or the income from parishes which did not require much exertion from them, men who could appreciate the significance of such a dictionary as that planned and were glad to co-operate in the preparation of it.

It is amusing to see how far those engaged in the editing of the *Dictionary* were from realising the magnitude of the enterprise. In 1860 the editor thought that he could begin publication in two years; in 1879, when the Oxford Press agreed to publish the work, it was stipulated that the editor was to have 'ten years to complete the work in'. Actually, as we have seen, the first part did not appear until 1884, and the last one until 1928, forty-four years later.

It is hard to estimate the importance to a great enterprise of its leader. Perhaps if he had not taken charge, another man might have been quite as successful with it as he was. But there is a possibility that without him the whole undertaking would have collapsed. In this case, at any rate, there can be no doubt of the importance of the third editor. Coleridge had made a promising beginning but had died prematurely; not much progress had been made in editing during the eighteen years that Furnivall was in charge; if the next editor had not been able to organise a producing staff, fix upon the exact methods of presenting the material and get copy actually ready for the press, it is likely that interest in the enterprise would have decreased to such an extent that nothing would have come of it. Indeed, in 1874, the president of the Society, Alexander J. Ellis, the distinguished author of the pioneering study of early English pronunciation, said in his presidential address: 'One of our works . . . remains, and for some time may remain, merely one of those things we have tried to do', and he added that he was inclined to think that a society 'is less fitted to compile a dictionary than to get the materials collected'. From this moribund condition the *Dictionary* was rescued by its third editor, James A. H. Murray, a Scottish schoolmaster in his early forties. Evidently Murray had the ability to impress people, for though he had at that time published but little, after conferences with the officers of the Society and the delegates of the Oxford Press, which had agreed to finance and publish the work, he was appointed editor.

Murray aroused fresh enthusiasm for the enterprise, organised an editorial staff and within five years was able to produce the first part. In one other respect the Society was fortunate in its choice of editor: Murray was long-lived; he served as editor for thirty-eight years.

Maybe only an experienced lexicographer can appreciate what an achievement it was to establish the method of organisation and presentation of the material of the *Dictionary*, with scarcely any model for imitation – a method moreover which in all essentials was to prove quite satisfactory for the work of fifty years. The *Oxford Dictionary* is 'all of a piece'; an expert can distinguish some minor differences in the treatment of words in the earlier parts and the last, as he can between the work of one editor and another, but they are trifling.

For some years Murray with his staff of assistants did all the editing, and hence it was common practice to refer to the work as 'Murray's Dictionary'. As it turned out, Murray did edit nearly half of the whole work. From 1888, however, a second independent staff was at work on the *Dictionary*. The way in which the second editor was secured is a curious story, which reveals the open-mindedness of Murray. On the publication of Part One of the *Dictionary*, the editor of a London weekly turned over the review copy that he had received to a young man recently arrived in the English capital. Ill-health in his early life had prevented this man, whose name was Henry Bradley, from attending a university. By means of tutors, however, and his own adventures with books, Bradley had acquired remarkable erudition, especially in languages and early literature. His review showed such an understanding of the problems of English lexicography and such a grasp of its subject-matter that, after an interview with him, Murray asked him to join the staff of the *Dictionary*; after two years of work with Murray, Bradley began to edit independently with a separate staff, continuing in the work for thirty-five years. From 1901 a third staff worked under Dr (later Sir) William Alexander Craigie (1867–1957), and from 1914 a fourth group under Dr Charles Talbut Onions (1873–1965) was also engaged in editing.

I know of no more enjoyable intellectual activity than working on a dictionary. Unlike most research, lexicography rarely sends one on fruitless quests; one does not devote days, months, or even years to testing an hypothesis only to decide that it is not tenable, or to attempting to collect evidence to prove a theory only to have to conclude that sufficient facts are no longer in existence to clinch it. It does not make one's life anxious, nor build up hopes only to have them collapse. Every day one is confronted by new problems, usually small but absorbingly interesting; at the end of the day one feels healthily tired, but content in the thought that one has accomplished something and advanced the whole work towards its completion. It must have been fun to be engaged on the *Dictionary* say in 1914, that peaceful time before the first World War, when all four staffs were competing with each other, at times perhaps somewhat acidly but always stimulatingly. One can imagine Murray at work, his patriarchal beard giving him a benign not to say saintly aspect; Bradley with his bristling bush suggesting force; Craigie with his trim beard, wasting no movement and writing his beautiful script with a steel pen; and bright-eyed Onions proving by being clean-shaven that a lexicographer does not positively have to be bearded.

LATER DICTIONARIES OF THE OXFORD TYPE

Before the completion of the *Oxford Dictionary* Professor Craigie published an article in the *Transactions of the Philological Society* on the future of English lexicography. He pointed out the fact that it would be impossible to prepare and publish a second edition of the great work because of the prohibitive cost, and argued that progress in English historical lexicography could be made by the compilation of dictionaries of more limited scope. He suggested the following fields: older and later Scottish, Middle English, and early Modern English. Craigie himself undertook *A Dictionary of the Older Scottish Tongue*, which began publication in 1931 but is still unfinished. During one summer he taught at the University of Chicago. In preparing one of his examinations at the end of the term it occurred to him to ask his students how they would plan a dictionary of American English. The idea, thus casually conceived, grew upon him and those with whom he discussed it. So he resigned his Oxford professorship and accepted a call to Chicago to teach and to edit a dictionary of American English. This dictionary was completed in 1944. In the *Scottish* dictionary he had to operate practically alone; but in the *American* dictionary he had the co-operation of a co-editor and an adequate staff. Approximately nineteen years were devoted to this dictionary, roughly half to the collection of material, half to editing it.

The Scottish National Dictionary was planned to supplement the *Older Scottish* by dealing with Scottish from about 1700. It began publication in 1931 under the editorship of William Grant. The fact that publication of the Scottish dictionaries has been slow is due to interruptions caused by the second World War. Dictionaries of Middle English and early Modern English have been undertaken; indeed work on the *Middle English Dictionary* was started before Craigie's article appeared; it has proceeded with but little interruption to the present time, and in December of 1952 the first part appeared. All of these dictionaries are on the Oxford plan, historical in aim, using dated quotations and plotting the development and interrelation of meanings. Those that have been published have been able to supplement significantly the information provided by *The Oxford English Dictionary*. This is true particularly of the *Dictionary of American English*, since, in the preparation of *The Oxford English Dictionary*, naturally emphasis was placed chiefly on English evidence. This dictionary has been followed by *A Dictionary of Americanisms*, which is in part based on it. This work, prepared, as the *D.A.E.* was, at the University of Chicago and edited by Dr Mitford M. Mathews, who was on the staff of the *D.A.E.*, has in some respects a narrower scope, in others a wider one. In particular it omits many words which are in the older book for cultural-historical reasons but which are not distinctly American, and it brings down the evidence as nearly as possible to the present time, thus adding many entries which, because of chronological limits, could not be included in the *D.A.E.* On the other hand, space considerations compelled the omission of many quotations. Like *The Century Dictionary*, this dictionary has illustrations; and, unlike the *D.A.E.*, it indicates pronunciation.

This is enough, I should think, by way of history of English dictionaries. It touches only the high points, the works which have contributed in some positive way to English lexicography. Dozens of dictionaries which have appeared are not named. Usually these are practical books, publishers' projects put together for ready sale. Some of these have had a considerable history, although their names would mean nothing to most people today. Thus in 1844 Alex Reid published a dictionary which went through at least twenty-five editions, appearing as late as 1877; and P. Austin Nuttall published a revision of Johnson in 1853, of Walker in 1859, and in 1863 a dictionary which he said was based 'on the labours of Worcester, Richardson, Webster' and six others (896 pages) which appeared in various abridgements and revisions as late as 1929–32.

MAKING A DICTIONARY

1. *Deciding its scope*

Perhaps the first step in making a dictionary is the determination of its scope, which may be dependent on the class of people for whom it is intended – if it is designed for a particular public, such as students in school, stenographers in offices; or only on its field, for example American English or dialects. Thus if the book is meant for school use it is likely that hosts of technical terms which are entered in the large dictionaries will be omitted; perhaps the range of words to be covered will be decided in large part by the frequency of occurrence in some word count, like those used in the *Thorndike-Century* dictionaries. In addition, obsolete words if found in the writings of Walter Scott, Shakespeare, Milton or other earlier English classics will be included because such texts may be assigned by teachers. On the other hand, a book for office use probably would omit such words but include many technical terms of trade and manufactures and such scientific terms as might come within the field of business. The policy of the dictionary on these and other matters, such as the use and nature of illustrations, will probably be determined in editorial conferences, in which the publisher also may take part.

In the case of the *Oxford Dictionary*, as we have seen, the paper prepared by Dean Trench was one of the earliest moves leading to decision on the scope and policies of that monumental work. No doubt the ideas presented there were worked over in many a conference before editing was begun. Determination of the method of presenting variant spellings, the classification and arrangement of meanings, the number of quotations for each meaning, etc., had to be made. One important decision was not to include the Anglo-Saxon vocabulary except in the case of words which survive into Middle English, but in such cases to give the Anglo-Saxon evidence to an extent proportionate with that of the other periods of English linguistic history.

It was especially difficult to define the scope of the material to be included in the *Dictionary of American English*. Obviously it was not desirable to duplicate uselessly material which was available in *The Oxford English Dictionary*; on the other hand, it was essential not to omit anything that was significant for the cultural life of the United States or its linguistic usage (no effort was made to include Canada, or of course anything south of the Rio Grande; to that extent the title is a misnomer due to the lack, in our language, of an adjective corresponding to the noun *United States*). Finally it was decided to include the names of all plants, animals, institutions which exist in the United States, all words which seemed possibly to have originated in the United States or to have been introduced there from foreign sources, and all words which had meanings not in use in Great Britain; in that case only the American meanings were given. In addition, to keep the work within manageable limits, it was decided to include no slang for which there was no evidence before 1875, no new locutions introduced after 1900, and no quotations later than 1925. Etymologies were given only for Americanisms, or where it seemed that the *Oxford* etymology was wrong. Similarly pronunciation was ignored except when a real contribution could be made. Finally, devices were adopted for indicating the relation of the entries to British usage (especially the date of the earliest appearance of the words in English), and in the case of words not in the best use, their status in American English. By such methods it was possible to get much more information into the space available than could have been done otherwise.

2. *The dictionary's use of earlier authorities*

Having fixed the scope of the work and many of its methods, the editor or editors are ready to begin. Perhaps most people who use a dictionary suppose that every such book starts from scratch – that its maker begins with a quire of blank paper and out of his inner consciousness writes down words, etymologies, definitions, etc., with no other knowledge of the entries in preceding dictionaries than what his memory may hold. Even brief consideration of the lexicographer's situation, however, should make it clear that he could not work in that way. The mind of no man or committee of men could bring forth on demand the wealth of knowledge presented by a good modern dictionary; if a book ever were put together in that way it would be such a poor thing that no one would look at it except in a spirit of fun. Indeed the relative perfection of the best modern dictionaries is due to the fact that they are the result of many minds working over many years.

We have noticed that Johnson used Bailey and that Webster used Johnson. Study of earlier dictionaries shows that they regularly built on their predecessors. For commercial reasons it is natural that customarily dictionaries should minimise or even deny their use of competing books; thus in his American edition Worcester expressly stated that he had not used Webster, though the title page of his English edition reads: 'Compiled from the Materials of Noah Webster'; apparently the English publishers thought that there was commercial advantage in the use of Webster's name! A more honest practice has been growing up, however: that of securing the right to use a preceding book and acknowledge the fact of such use. Thus the *Century* acknowledged the use of Ogilvie's dictionary; i.e. Annandale's enlargement. More recently the General Introduction of *The American College Dictionary* states that the editors have used the *Century* and the *Dictionary of American English*, and in a note on the back of the title page acknowledgement is made of use of several technical dictionaries.

Whether such explicit acknowledgement is made or not, anyone who consults a dictionary can be sure that its editor has considered what appears in preceding books of the kind and in his competitors, and used as much of it as seemed to him desirable for his own book. Even the most expert, most widely informed lexicographer, equipped with the most nearly complete body of evidence, would not dare to risk overlooking some bit of information valuable to his work; he must make sure that his rival has not included something important which has escaped him.

In addition to such information and ideas as he can get from his predecessors, the lexicographer frequently has collections of material valuable for his work which have been published in one form or another. Thus the *Dictionary of American English* could use several volumes on American vocabulary and specifically American meanings of words, notably those published by J. R. Bartlett, whose book passed through three editions, and by R. H. Thornton, whose collections of quotations derived from his systematic reading of the *Congressional Record* and other sources proved of the greatest value. The Preface to the *D.A.E.* acknowledges indebtedness to *The Oxford English Dictionary* and to the books on Americanisms, but not to the *Century* or *Webster's*, which of course were used constantly. Similarly the *Middle English Dictionary* has in addition to two inadequate predecessor dictionaries, the Chaucer concordance and the glossaries of texts of many Middle English writings.

Finally, the lexicographer has at hand general reference books such as works on plants, animals, and political institutions. Of course in addition he will consult many a book in a reference collection such as that in a college or university library for information on subjects connected with his entries.

3. *New material used in dictionary-making*

The essential material for any dictionary of the *Oxford* type, however, is of course the mass of quotations which have been collected for it. Volunteer unpaid readers contributed millions of quotations to the *Oxford Dictionary*; members of the staff also contributed large numbers; much the same is true of the *Middle English Dictionary*, for it has been stated that a hundred volunteers read for it. A commercial dictionary also collects quotations, especially of new words or meanings; certain members of the staff spend most of their time reading current publications in order to obtain such evidence of new additions to the English vocabulary.

4. *Spelling*

The first task of the editor of a dictionary is to decide on the spelling of his word-entry. Usually on a modern dictionary this affords no difficulty, as usage has fixed a single spelling as the only correct one. No other element in the lexicographer's subject-matter is so rigid or so without system or reason as spelling. Attention has been called frequently to the fact that in some instances there are many ways of spelling the same sound in English, e.g. *reef, thief, deceive, mere, people, beat, encyclopaedia, amoeba, ravine, quay*; that there are several phonetic values for some letters, e.g. *hat, hate, all*; and that there are hosts of silent letters, e.g. final *e*'s, the *p* in *pneumonia*, the *b* in *crumb*, the *l* in *talk*, the *k* in *know*. In the teaching of spelling in the schools, efforts are made to reduce the irregularities to a series of rules or categories, but in a language which offers such situations as that found in words which end in *-ough* (*cough, dough, through, tough, drought*), any classifications must be at best merely approximate.

The fact is that English spelling did not develop in any orderly way; indeed the whole story of modern English spelling is so complicated and irregular that there existed no satisfactory book on the subject until G. H. Vallins's *Spelling* appeared in 1954, with a chapter by John W. Clark on American spelling. Until near the end of the fourteenth century, spelling was essentially phonetic, each letter having a single sound, that of the Latin alphabet. This was not a perfect system; for example, long and short vowels were represented by the same letter, though sometimes a scribe used a doubled letter to indicate a long vowel, which was distinctive enough. At the same time different spellings of the same word indicated differences in pronunciation, usually differences characteristic of various parts of the country, or, in other words, of dialects. Thus our *merry* would be spelt *meri, muri, miri*, to represent the pronunciation of different localities.

D

From about 1400 on, English spelling and the pronunciation of cultivated people all over England tended to approximate the usage of London. This spelling is essentially that of a good modern edition of Chaucer. There is a logical relation here, for Chaucer was a Londoner of the last half of the fourteenth century whose pronunciation (and presumably his spelling, for that would represent his pronunciation) must have been those of well-bred London people. Not long after Chaucer's death, however, the final e found on many words in fourteenth-century speech, and the e in the ending es, ceased to be pronounced, and other changes occurred, e.g. the sound represented by gh, which was approximately that of German ch, was replaced by some other consonant or dropped entirely. Likewise a series of changes affecting all the long vowels began. These changes occurred, but because of the influence of the spelling of early fifteenth-century manuscripts and of printing, which was based on that of such fourteenth-century documents as the writings of Chaucer and Gower and the manuscripts of *Piers Plowman*, the spelling of the fourteenth century was retained unaltered.

The resulting divorce of spelling from sound was increased by the introduction of many foreign words, especially French and Latin, with retention of the spelling of those languages, regardless of how the words were pronounced. Some consciousness of the confusion existing in English spelling led to efforts at improvement, which unfortunately took the form of respelling according to Latin standards or those of some language from which it was supposed that the word was derived. Thus a d was introduced into words like *adventure* which were adapted from French where the Latin d had been lost, and even into words like *advance* and *advantage* which had not had a d in Latin. In those instances spelling has influenced pronunciation, but not in cases like *scissors* and *schism*, not to speak of *scent* which had no c anywhere until the seventeenth century and must have got it somehow from words like *scissors* and *scene*. Other instances are *isle*, which had no etymological connection with *island* but caused s to be added to the longer word, and *delight*, which is not related to *light*. Probably the anomalous eo in *people* (derived from French *peuple*) was due to an effort to make it look like Latin *populus*; and maybe the *ue* on *tongue* is due to French *langue*, which at least has the same meaning even if it is obviously quite a different word. Later when new words were introduced from foreign sources the original spelling was retained, however they were pronounced, e.g. *psychology*, *pthisis*, *connoisseur*. A glance at printed books of the fifteenth and sixteenth centuries will show that then it was still possible to spell the same word in more than one way; and even as late as the seventeenth century many spellings which are not those of our fixed spelling occur. Thus in a page of a folio history of England dedicated to King James I (1627) I find: *bloud* (for blood), *forraine* (for foreign), *imployment*, *trayterous*, *divel* (devil), *farre* (far), *cloake*, *sonne* (son), *hoast* (host). Gradually, however, the notion that a word ought always to be spelt in the same way developed. Perhaps experience convinced master printers and publishers that unless their journeymen had a positive model to follow the page exhibited a chaos which was offensive to the public. Just how, before the appearance of comprehensive dictionaries, the norm was made apparent to the printers is not clear, perhaps by the compilation of something in the nature of an embryonic style book. After Bailey's dictionary was available, still more after Johnson's had appeared, of course it was possible to set that book as a standard for spelling. To what extent Bailey or Johnson made conscious selection among variant spellings I do not know; as far as I am aware there has been no study of that point. Johnson says that he chose the spelling which seemed to him in widest use. At any rate, there never was any systematic effort to iron out the inconsistencies in the spelling of any dictionary. Until Noah Webster appeared on the scene, lexicographers spelt as the printed books of their time did, at most merely settling on one of two or more spellings then in vogue and that the one which seemed to them the most widely used.

Noah Webster, however, would have liked to institute a thorough reform of English spelling. Before bringing out any of his dictionaries, he published proposals for extensive revision and regulation of spelling, especially urging the omission of superfluous letters like the *ue* on *tongue*, the *b* on *thumb*, the *ugh* on *though*. He met with vigorous opposition, as all later efforts in this direction have done. Consequently he introduced relatively few reformed spellings into his dictionaries and, with the exception of some types of simplification, these were removed from his work after his death. His corrections did win favour in some categories of words; and to him Americans at least owe relief from the *u* in *honor, labor*, etc., the *k* on words like *music* and the regularisation of the *er, re* ending in favour of *er*.

Since English usage did not accept all of those corrections which American usage accepted from Webster (it did strike out the *k* on *music* and similar words) and because for no known reason there are sporadic differences between British and American spelling, e. g. *kerb, curb; tyre, tire; gaol, jail*, the English lexicographer will spell a few entries differently from the American, but both will give the two spellings, marking them so as to indicate their national provenience. In the main the maker of an ordinary dictionary experiences little difficulty with spelling. Even when two spellings are in use, e.g. *Renaissance, Renascence; catsup, ketchup*, it is not greatly important which is used in the entry, though some people who consult may interpret the chosen spelling as evidence of decided preference; both spellings must be given and also a cross-reference.

Though commercial dictionaries and some special historical dictionaries such as the *Dictionary of American English* and *A Dictionary of Americanisms* need devote little thought to spelling, the *Oxford Dictionary* did have difficulty with one class of words: those which have become obsolete. The policy adopted was to use for the entry the last recorded spelling. This decision was not too happy, though it would not have occasioned much trouble if extensive cross-referencing had been permitted. Probably cost was the chief reason for not making sufficient cross-references. In working with the book, I have often felt that poor judgment was used in the whole matter, that sometimes references are given when with a modicum of thought one could have found the desired word without any reference, and that in others none is given when it could not reasonably be expected that anyone could find the desired word. In fact the reader who wants information on an obsolete word must use all his ingenuity in trying to surmise the spelling used in the last quotation which the *Oxford* editor had. Many a person – even a trained scholar carrying on research – has to conclude that a word is not in *O.E.D.* when it actually is there under a spelling he could not divine. *The Oxford English Dictionary* has within its boards an excellent Middle English dictionary, as the clever editors of some Middle English texts have shown by the elucidation of rare words which they have been able to get from it; but many who have tried to find Middle English words in it have not had the intellectual agility to locate them and have given up with the statement that the word is not in *O.E.D.* The *Middle English Dictionary* now in process of publication is faced with a grievous problem in the determination of the spellings of entries because of the great variety of spellings in different dialects and at different times. I must say that I can see no way out except by the use of thousands of cross-references.

One final note on spelling. *The Oxford English Dictionary* gives for words that have been long in the language a record of spellings by centuries, by means of which one can see at a glance the history of the spelling of those words. Some pages back I said that the *c* in *scent* was not found till the seventeenth century; that fact I obtained from the scheme of spellings in *O.E.D.* Opening the book at random, I came upon *Satiric* and learn that the early spellings were *satyryke, satyricque, satyrick, satyryque, satyric,* and that the first instance of *satiric* was not found till the eighteenth century. As in many instances in the history of English spelling, there has been effective simplification. Would that there could have been such simplification regularly!

5. *Pronunciation*

Having devoted probably only a moment's thought to the spelling of his entry, the dictionary man can pass to what is usually placed next – pronunciation. The *Oxford Dictionary*, like all commercial dictionaries, had to give information which would enable those who used it to pronounce words correctly. The *Dictionary of American English*, however, since its aim was chiefly historical, paid no attention to pronunciation, whereas *A Dictionary of Americanisms*, whose interest is perhaps as much contemporary as historical, has taken great pains with it.

In any general dictionary, however, the duty to give attention to pronunciation is inescapable. But unhappily it offers problems which no one has been able to solve satisfactorily, e.g. to what extent to present differences between English and American pronunciations, what variety of British English to regard as standard for England, and whether to include other British pronunciations, similarly which of two or more pronunciations current in America to include, and to what extent to include their provenience. There are certain situations for which general statements can be made, such as the treatment of final *r* and *r* before a consonant in different areas of the United States. The dictionary that one uses is likely to make some observation concerning these situations in a preliminary section on pronunciation. Thus in *The American College Dictionary* Professor Greet writes that the pronunciation indicated is 'subject always to the speech ways that are standard in the major regions. For instance, as in all American dictionaries, *r* after vowels is included in the phonetic respelling but without the expectation or desire that southern and north-eastern Americans should change their pronunciation of words like *father*.' Now of course it would be redundant and space-consuming to give two pronunciations and indicate their provenience every time a word containing an *r* in this position turned up; but I wonder how many users of our dictionaries realise that when they see *färthar*, they are to understand that in the case of Virginians it means *fätha*? If they do I should think they might wonder how much value there is in the dictionary's respelling. Nor does *O.E.D.* or the *Merriam-Webster* give more guidance. Most dictionaries make an effort to distinguish between English and American pronunciation when they are aware of any. But the attempt sometimes results in uncertainty in the reader's mind. For example, *The American College Dictionary* gives the pronunciation of *either* as 'ēthar or esp. Brit. īthar'. From that one would conclude that the second pronunciation is current in England but could only guess as to the extent of its use there or in the United States. As presumably everyone has heard both pronunciations in the United States, an American gains really nothing from the entry, and an Englishman would learn only what the American knows to begin with. As is to be expected from its larger size, *Merriam-Webster* gives more information, chiefly about the history of British pronunciation, but makes no effort to indicate the distribution of the two pronunciations in the United States. The *O.E.D.* gives a more satisfactory account of the history of the two chief pronunciations in England and the present condition there, but nothing whatever on the United States! It must be admitted that on pronunciation dictionaries are less satisfactory than on spelling, meaning, or etymology.

Moreover there is considerable difference at times in the pronunciations recommended by reputable dictionaries. This sort of thing is shown effectively in a list of the 1934 *Merriam-Webster* entitled 'Synopsis of words differently pronounced by different orthoepists'. The dictionaries used are: *Oxford* (to which is added the *Concise Oxford* when that abridgement has altered the pronunciation indicated in the parent work), a pronouncing dictionary edited by the distinguished English phonetician Daniel Jones, the *Universal Dictionary* of Professor H. C. Wyld of Oxford, the *Century*, the *Standard*, and the pronunciations of English words in a French-English dictionary prepared by the late George Hempl, long a notable scholar in English philology in American universities. Of course the different books do not disagree completely in all cases listed. Thus for *banal*, *Merriam-Webster* includes practically all the pronunciations advocated by the other dictionaries. But one finds interest in learning that *O.E.D.*, *Century* and *Standard* allow only pronunciations which stress the first syllable. Of *been* one sees little of moment except that Wyld countenances only the one with the long vowel, which is rarely heard in the United States and then perhaps only as a spelling pronunciation or one imitated from British usage. Sometimes the only disagreement is that the British dictionaries do not recognise American pronunciation, as when Wyld and Jones give for *afford, afod*, though in the United States of course an *r* would be uttered in a territory so large that the characteristics of it are now called General American. Still, the nineteen pages of this list provide many striking instances of differences in the judgment of recent lexicographers.

The dictionary-maker of today does not need to rely on his own judgment in recording pronunciation; he is happy enough in being able to turn over that responsibility to an expert. In England Professor Daniel Jones has published a pronouncing dictionary of cultivated Southern British English; in the United States Professor John S. Kenyon, who acted as consulting editor for pronunciation on the last edition of *Merriam-Webster*, has published a book on American pronunciation, and, with the late Thomas A. Knott, a dictionary of American pronunciation. In *The American College Dictionary* Professor W. Cabell Greet was in charge of the subject. Editors in charge of pronunciation consult other scholars on particular points of difficulty as a matter of course.

The method of showing pronunciation in most commercial dictionaries is extremely clumsy, but it seems to satisfy the general public. It consists of respelling words, immediately after the entries, according to a system of letter values, which it is hoped will make clear to the reader how the words are pronounced. For the vowel letters the value they have predominantly in English spelling is used as basis: thus *a*, with appropriate diacritical marks, represents the sounds of *a* in *hat* or *hate*. No doubt these values seem natural to the English-speaking world, though in no other language, as far as I know, has *a* the significance of what in English is called the long *a* sound. Unfortunately in order to make the five vowel letters express the much larger number of vowel sounds in English it is necessary to use many diacritical marks; indeed so many that it is hopeless for me to attempt to remember the meaning of some of them. Evidently others have the same trouble, for it is customary for dictionaries to print at the bottom of each page or 'opening', key words containing the letters with the marks. Obviously it would be better to use a phonetic alphabet in which each letter would always correspond to the same sound and each sound would be represented by the same letter. Such an alphabet exists – indeed many alphabets of the sort have been devised – and has had wide use among scholars and teachers of foreign languages; it is the alphabet of the International Phonetic Association. With some slight modifications this has been used in some dictionaries, notably the *Oxford* and *A Dictionary of Americanisms*. It was even used as an alternate means of indicating pronunciation in the *Standard Dictionary* and still appears in the latest printings of that book (although not in the abridged forms), but I doubt that the great advantage in this respect of the *Standard* over *Webster's* is appreciated by most dictionary users. It is not difficult to learn, but probably the fact that it includes some letters not part of the English alphabet and perhaps its association of familiar letters with sounds not commonly so represented in English, e.g. *ai* for the English long *i*, and *i* for the accented vowel in *police*, makes it uncongenial to the general public. There is no way out of these difficulties, because there are many more than twenty-six sounds in our language. Anyway, the public probably is not conscious of the fact that the conventional respelling is clumsy and bothersome; it expects to look at the bottom of the page and work out the meaning of the respelling.

6. *Etymology*

In the arrangement which used to be standard in dictionaries, the next item to which the editor turns is the etymology of his entry; in some practical dictionaries of recent date, this has been relegated to a position at the end of the entry, and in the case of small books omitted entirely. These last-mentioned practices are defensible enough, for to most readers information about the sources of words is as dry as dust, a pedantic matter of no possible consequence. Probably not once in a thousand consultations of a dictionary is finding out the etymology any part of the purpose. Indeed it is doubtful that the average person who looks up a word for any reason notices the etymology or would understand it if he did. Clearly in giving such information lexicographers are following their own scholarly bent and not considering the needs of their public. To them, as men interested in words, origins are important, indeed indispensable for a true understanding of words. But the unfavourable attitude toward etymology is so strong that it has been suggested to me that in this book I minimise it or omit the subject altogether. Yet, oddly enough, when judiciously mixed with details about developments in meaning and analogical association with other words affecting the spelling or meaning of words, etymology is a prime ingredient in a concoction that can be made appetising to many people. Discursive books which do not have to treat every word in the language but can pick those which the writer sees ways of making interesting, have a wide sale. We have seen that as far back as the middle of the nineteenth century Dean Trench published books of this sort which had vogue. Later Greenough and Kittredge published, in magazines, articles which eventually formed a book, *Words and their Ways in English Speech*. Then the late Professor Ernest Weekley had success with a number of such books; and most recently the English journalist Ivor Brown has produced a series of small books which have pleased the general public in England and America, and Eric Partridge has published several books on idiosyncrasies of English etymology and English usage.

In truth etymology is important and interesting, not only because vestiges of the original meanings of words often remain in present senses (e.g. one conscious of the etymology of *virile* will use it of a woman only humorously or pejoratively), but also because the origins of words reveal much that is significant in the cultural history of our people. There are two general possibilities in English etymology: one that the word is descended from the stock of words which formed the vocabulary of the Angles and Saxons who conquered Britain in the fifth century. These were simple, unlettered folk concerned in thought, experience, and speech only with the minimum essentials of daily living. Long ago Sir Walter Scott publicised a point made earlier by a commentator on languages: that the names of domestic animals are derived from Anglo-Saxon but that those of dressed meats were borrowed from French, an indication that in early England the preparation of meat for cooking was inferior to that introduced by the French-speaking invaders under William the Conqueror. Again, whereas *father, mother, son, daughter, brother* and *sister* belong to the primitive stock, the names of more remote relatives are French: *niece, nephew, uncle, aunt, cousin*. Evidently such relationships were not much in the minds of our ancient ancestors, although sister's son was, as even one whose reading is chiefly in comparatively late literature would expect from one's knowledge of ballads.

The other chief possibility, of course, is that the word has been introduced from some foreign source. Always in such cases the significance of the etymology is that it reveals cultural indebtedness to the nation from whose language the word was taken; not only the word but the idea or object named, or the attitude which the word expresses, was imported from abroad. Thus the borrowing of the word *castle* was made because there were no stone castles in Anglo-Saxon England, and so when the Norman barons began to erect them they were referred to by the French name. All the titles of nobility except *lord* and *earl* and most words concerned with government (not *alderman*) and law were borrowed from French because the cultural elements which they name were foreign to Anglo-Saxon civilisation. For similar reasons, of words of religion only *God* is part of the original stock, despite the fact that the words were introduced before the end of the Anglo-Saxon period because England was Christianised in the seventh and eighth centuries. Of a different sort, the word *naïve* expresses judgment revealing an attitude of a somewhat subtle nature which probably did not exist in England until it was introduced from French culture with the word in the seventeenth century.

Further, with the information provided by the *Oxford Dictionary* as to the date of the earliest quotations that have been found, we can tell more or less exactly when words and the things or ideas which they name became a part of English culture. It was this information which gave me the authority to make the observation about *naïve* in the preceding paragraph. Further, the names of some musical instruments such as *piano*, and of forms of poetry such as *sonnet* and *madrigal*, were brought into English from Italian as part of the well-known Italianate influence upon English culture; but some of them came through French, e.g. *spinet* – an indication that France acted as mediator. The fact that *algebra* is originally Arabic is evidence that England got that form of mathematics from Arabic culture, in part perhaps directly through books and the experience of English students in Spanish (Moorish) universities, but in part also indirectly through France and Italy, both of which used the word and the study.

The fact that for most words correct etymologies can be given now is a result not of lexicographical work but of the study of linguistic history. Scholars had to discover the historical inter-relation of languages and the exact sound correspondences between one language and another before it was possible to determine whether one word was related to another, and if it was, in just what way. Thus, before the sound developments of the different languages had been discovered, a person who noted the rough similarity between English *father* and Latin *pater*, English *mother* and Latin *mater* might suppose that the English words were derived from the Latin ones. Now because of our knowledge of phonetic laws we know that the words are related, to be sure, but as brothers not as parents and children. Noah Webster made a great effort to improve Johnson's etymologies but failed in the main because he had not perceived the historical relations of languages.

Careful study of the vocabulary of most languages in Europe and a few in Asia and of the correspondences of sounds in obviously related words has shown that these languages have developed from a common source which no longer exists, the hypothetical Indo-European language. That it no longer exists is by no means surprising, for it must have been in use long before the invention of writing and hence was never recorded in stone inscription, clay tablet, or manuscript. The descendants of this long-dead language were languages themselves dead but sometimes surviving in written form, e.g. Latin and Sanskrit, sometimes not wholly lost but represented by living languages which derived from them, e.g. Albanian. Just how this develop-ment occurred we can see from what happened in the case of Latin; from that language came the modern Romance lan-guages, French, Italian, Spanish, etc. In like manner English, German, the Scandinavian languages, etc., derived from one ancestor, no longer extant and probably never written down, the hypothetical Germanic language. Each of these groups of languages has its phonetic peculiarities, sound changes which differentiate it from the other Indo-European languages, differences in endings and in vocabulary, and each individual language has peculiarities which distinguish it from the other members of its group. Obviously this matter is extremely complicated; and naturally it took a long time for the host of scholars who worked at it to establish even the more general correspondences. But the final effect was that it was, is, possible to discern with certainty the etymological relations of most words. Let us see how this knowledge works.

One of the characteristic features of the Germanic languages is that they agree in displaying systematically a certain series of consonants which in long lists of words correspond to a different series in the other Indo-European languages. Consequently it is supposed that the Indo-European sounds were changed to the corresponding sounds in primitive Germanic. That surmise is of no consequence for the etymologist, however; the essential point is that the correspondences are exact and invariable. The list of correspondences is called Grimm's law from the name of the German scholar who is familiar to all of us as one of the brothers Grimm of folk-tale fame, and who publicised these sound relations in his Germanic grammar. It is not necessary to give all the details of Grimm's law; a few examples will suffice to show how such sound laws make the work of the etymologist sure. According to Grimm's law, Indo-European *t* (as in Latin, Greek, etc.) corresponds to Þ (the sound represented in modern English by *th*, as in *thin* rather than in *this*); *d* corresponds to *t* in Germanic. Suppose a person who knows some Latin and Greek wonders whether the words which mean *tooth* in those languages are related to English *tooth;* the stems of those words are *dent-* and *odont-*. According to Grimm's law the Indo-European *d* will be a *t* in Germanic and the *t* a Þ; so we substitute those sounds for the consonants found in Latin and Greek; the result is *tenÞ* or *tanÞ*, since every Indo-European short *o* became *a* in Germanic. The variation between *e* and *o*, it is known, is a characteristic of Indo-European; it amounts to this: different words or different inflectional forms of the same word may be built on the same root with *e* or *o* – a condition known in German and some English linguistic texts as *Ablaut*, in other English writing as *Gradation*. Since English has *o* in *tooth*, evidently it represents the same grade as the Greek word; so the Germanic form must have been *tanÞ* from *tonÞ*. Only one step remains; a characteristic of Anglo-Saxon is the loss of *n* before voiceless spirants, that is consonant sounds which can be prolonged as long as the breath holds out and which are not voiced, e.g. *s, f, Þ*; and when the *n* has dropped there is 'compensatory lengthening', i.e. the vowel is lengthened; hence we reach the form actually found in Anglo-Saxon, *tōÞ*. Anglo-Saxon *ō* regularly becomes *oo*; so we have *tooth*.

It is a certainty that our *tooth* is a word which Anglo-Saxon inherited from Indo-European and that it is a cousin, or in technical terms a cognate, to the Greek and Latin words. But what about *dentist*, which has the same consonants as Latin? As that does not have the Germanic consonants, clearly it is not a Germanic word but is borrowed or rather made up from the Latin word. On consulting the *Oxford* dictionary one is not surprised to learn that it does not appear in English until the eighteenth century.

The last sentence illustrates one important service that lexicography did perform to etymology – the establishment of the approximate date of the introduction of borrowed words into the language. The information is important in etymology as a check on any surmise as to the source of a word. It is said commonly that there are three essentials for a correct etymology: (1) differences in sounds between a word and its supposed source must be explainable by known phonetic laws (of this our consideration of *tooth* may serve as an example); (2) there must be a reasonable relationship of meaning; (3) in the case of borrowing there must be historical contact between the two cultures at the time when the assumed borrowing occurred. No etymologist now would suggest that English derived a word directly from the language of a country with which the English nation had no connection either by actual physical contact such as commerce or travel, or by books or other forms of writing. Hence the importance in etymology of knowing when the word was introduced into the language.

From the time of Queen Elizabeth I on, there were antiquarians who studied Anglo-Saxon. Indeed in the seventeenth and eighteenth centuries, dictionaries, naturally very imperfect, of that oldest form of English were published. By use of them it was possible for anyone sufficiently interested in the history of words to find and recognise the sources of such modern words as *mother* (A.S. *modor*), *think* (A.S. *þencan*), *ride* (A.S. *ridan*), *do* (A.S. *don*). Further, an acquaintance with Latin, possessed by most educated Englishmen, made recognition of the debt to Latin in such words as *deprivation, census, pauper*, obvious. Similarly the introduction into English of French words could not fail to be noticed. On the basis of such evidence a man like Bailey, who made the first attempt to explain the etymology of all English words, could give many correct sources of English words in his dictionary. Of course in a host of instances this sort of knowledge did not suffice; and faulty assumptions were made; but with no scientific understanding of the inter-relations of languages and of the dates when words were introduced into English, there was no way of avoiding such errors. Macaulay's account of Johnson in the *Encyclopædia Britannica* is unjust to that great man when he says:

> The faults of the book resolve themselves, for the most part, into one great fault. Johnson was a wretched etymologist. He knew little or nothing of any Teutonic language except English, which indeed, as he wrote it, was scarcely a Teutonic language; and thus he was absolutely at the mercy of Junius and Skinner (authors of etymological dictionaries).

Actually in the state of knowledge of the history of languages which prevailed in Johnson's time and even in Webster's no one could have made dependable etymologies, though it should be stressed that the mass of Johnson's etymologies are correct. Noah Webster saw the need of improvement in etymology, and to that end he studied some twenty languages and tried to form a science of linguistics. It is not surprising if one man could not accomplish, in the midst of a busy life, what it took a series of German scholars working for half a century from the early eighteen hundreds on to establish. Some improvement was made in later dictionaries, but really scientific etymologies were not available until 1879–82. In these years Professor W. W. Skeat published his *Etymological Dictionary*, which utilised the scientific knowledge of linguistics gained in the preceding decades chiefly in Germany. In his introduction Skeat states that a chief motive for making his dictionary was to be of help to *The Oxford English Dictionary*. The editors, themselves able scholars of historical linguistics, could use Skeat's etymologies with such additions and corrections as their own knowledge enabled them to make.

The *Merriam-Webster* of 1864 employed the German scholar, Dr C. A. F. Mahn, for the etymological work. On his death Professor E. S. Sheldon of Harvard, probably the greatest Romance philologist of his time, and one of the gentlest, most modest and open-minded of scholars, was engaged to continue the work. Because of the foundation laid by Mahn and Sheldon, the etymologies in late *Merriam-Websters* are the best to be found in any one dictionary; of course the *O.E.D.* with its larger scale often gives more details. Though the *Standard Dictionary* reduced the space devoted to etymologies because of its understanding that the public cares little for the derivation of words, it engaged Professor F. A. March, a man of some standing in academic life, to oversee that feature. More recently, *The American College Dictionary* engaged Professor Kemp Malone of Johns Hopkins to edit its etymologies. More recently still, Eric Partridge has given us *Origins*, an etymological dictionary (first published in 1958, revised in a fourth edition in 1966) of the commonest words in modern English. By means of a readily intelligible system of cross-references the author of this unique work has contrived to group nearly and distantly related words together and to expound their histories simply and clearly.

7. *Meanings*

Though the modern lexicographer may depute to others the responsibility of determining the pronunciations and etymologies which are to appear in his dictionary, he must wrestle with the meanings himself; and the task may be extremely complicated and difficult. Perhaps in some happy primitive time each word in a language had only one meaning, but in extant languages, even dead ones like Latin or Greek, many words have several, and at times a large number of meanings. To be sure, in the ordinary course of daily life we are hardly conscious of this fact. We speak of the trunk of a tree, of an elephant, or of the specially made box in which we pack our personal possessions when we travel, without consciousness that we are using one word in entirely different senses. Actually the surroundings in which we use the word, its context as people say, make the meaning of the word so sure that we do not think of the fact that it has different senses. Sometimes we do by chance use a word in a context in which it might have different meanings, or in a context in which a homophone, i.e. a word pronounced the same though historically of different origin, e.g. *see*, *sea*, (the Holy) *See*, would make sense; in such cases we are likely to smile and perhaps spell the word that we mean. Puns are intentional uses of words with ambiguity of this sort.

The reason for the development of several senses for one word is that as civilisation or culture advances, a need for means of expressing many new ideas, naming new products, expressing new kinds of action arises; and the method used in increasing the range of word-meanings is chiefly not the invention of new words but the addition of new meanings to words already in the language. The way that this is done is to employ some established word in a figurative or transferred sense. In some instances the process is very obvious, e.g. when we use *foot* in such a phrase as *foot* of the class, probably we are conscious that we are using a word meaning the part of the human body which is at the end of the leg, in a transferred sense; similarly when we speak of *footing* a bill; but in other cases there is more or less complete dissociation of the word from its original meaning; thus when I mention *foot* as a measure of length, what is in my mind is the idea of twelve inches or a third of a yard, not any figurative relation to the human foot. Whether there is any lingering realisation of figure or not, the proliferation of meanings in some cases is prodigious. Thus *body*, which of course originally meant only the physical organism of a plant or animal, has in *Merriam-Webster* twenty-nine meanings, e.g. a corpse, the main part of a building or of a document, consistency or thickness, a group of people (a legislative body), a mass of particulars (a body of facts).

The difficulty of discerning the different meanings and deter-

E

mining their logical arrangement and the time and energy which they require are inconceivable to anyone who has not worked on a historical dictionary. The maker of a commercial dictionary has a much easier job, since earlier lexicographers have established the principal meanings of the words, and he has merely to decide which ones come within his scope, whether any new ones should be added (here he uses the quotations which have been gathered for him), and whether to arrange them in an order different from that of his predecessors. The historical lexicographer must dig out the meanings represented in the stack of slips before him and arrange them in the historical order of their development, not in a simple 1, 2, 3 order either, but in a I, II, III arrangement with subordinate meanings under those main senses. In 1881 Murray wrote that one of the sub-editors of the *O.E.D.* had devoted forty hours to analysis of the meanings of the verb *set* – and commented that probably the editor would have to devote forty more hours to it. At that time there were fifty-one senses of the simple verb, and eighty-three of such phrases as *set out, set off*. As finally published in 1914, *set, v*(erb) had 126 meanings and twenty-six combinations with an adverb, of which the last, *set up*, had forty-four senses. Even in a more restricted dictionary like the *Dictionary of American English* there are twenty-five meanings of the verb *cut*. So the editor may have to devote many days to one word, or when the sense distinctions are few he may be able to edit several words in one day.

Perhaps the reader noticed that in 1881, three years before the appearance of the first part of *O.E.D.*, a sub-editor was engaged on a word as far along in the alphabet as *set*. Evidently there was an enormous amount of pre-editing on the *O.E.D.* before any part of it was in final form; superficially such procedure meant a great waste of time and energy; but it must be realised that as the editor and his assistants had no model for what they were to produce they had to make many attempts, many of them false no doubt, before they could arrive at the methods and forms which were satisfactory. It may be that the special problems of a particular historical dictionary may require much preliminary editing and re-editing, but now that general procedures have been worked out more economy of effort should be possible. Certainly the editing of the *Dictionary of American English* proceeded with hardly any false steps from the beginning straight to the completion of the work. Yet perhaps because of the unfortunate deaths of editors and hence the lack of continuity in the work, there has been much re-editing of the *Middle English Dictionary*.

The editor or sub-editor of a historical dictionary starts with a stack of slips which have been alphabetised by a junior member of the staff but otherwise are undigested. His first act is to discard slips which are not needed, duplicates, and quotations which for one reason or another fall outside the scope of his dictionary. In the case of *O.E.D.* these might be quotations of Anglo-Saxon words for which there were no quotations of later date; technical senses which seemed no part of the general vocabulary; and occasional instances of foreign words in an English environment but obviously felt to be foreign and represented by at most only a few sporadic occurrences. Similarly the editors of the *Dictionary of American English* discarded all quotations which on comparison with *O.E.D.* it was clear represented ordinary English usage, all technical words or meanings not in general use, all words for which there was no evidence before 1900, all slang words or uses not found before 1875 and all quotations later than 1925.

This preliminary sifting done, the editor separates the slips into small piles according to their meanings. There is no great mystery in this distinction of senses, though of course some people are more sensitive to such differences than others, and anyone who does not perceive them readily should not attempt lexicographical work. Still, it does not require great perspicacity in most cases. Consider the following quotations for *acute*: 'An acute angle is that which is less than a right angle'; 'It is plainly an acute distemper, and she cannot hold out three days'; 'Such a circumstance could not be lost upon so acute an observer'. Anyone, I should suppose, would realise that there are three distinct senses in those sentences.

As soon as the editor has separated his quotations, he may see that there is a gap in one or other of the groups of quotations, e.g. there is no quotation after the eighteenth century, though he knows that the word in that sense is commonly used still. If the lack is in the mathematical sense, he sends an assistant to look in a recent book on geometry and so obtains a quotation which fills out the evidence. Similarly if it is the medical sense, he has books on that subject searched. In the case of non-technical senses it may be quite difficult to find the needed example; nevertheless a clever assistant may come up with a quotation in no very long time. Some member of the staff is likely to develop almost an uncanny knack for discovering wanted quotations.

Sometimes all efforts to find the quotation needed for a word or meaning fail. In that case, the *D.A.E.*, if we were convinced that the word was valid, quotes the dictionary in which we found it. Recently I visited a place called Bartholomew's Cobble in Western Massachusetts. Curious as to just what *cobble* meant there, I looked it up in *Merriam-Webster* in vain, then in *D.A.E.* and found it there with only the *Century* as authority. On the other hand sometimes *O.E.D.*, lacking a quotation, inserts a characteristic sentence which its editors have heard people say, e.g. in the *Supplement* s.v. *set*, v., sense 141 *Mod[ern]*, 'That automobile will set some guy back a lot of dough'. The *D.A.E.* did not permit itself that liberty.

8. *Definitions*

The next task is the framing of the definitions for the several meanings. Of course everyone who has used a dictionary has some idea of the form and manner of the definitions used in such a book, and the editor, an experienced man, should be and probably is a master at devising them. A good definition is one that gives a clear unambiguous characterisation or explanation of the meaning or a meaning of a word. It does not use the word, or any word based on the same root, in defining itself. Thus if I had written: a good definition is one that defines the meaning of a word, I should have dodged the issue or begged the question. The reader would have got no real information, nothing that he did not know before he read my discussion. Yet such slipshod definitions find place in dictionaries. In what follows I shall use actual definitions given in dictionaries but shall alter inessential words so that it will not be apparent from what dictionary I have derived them. Thus *Negro* is defined as: 'An individual of the Negro race'. That would be acceptable only if *Negro race* were well defined, but in the dictionary which gives this definition there is no heading for *Negro race*. What is required is something like this: 'A member of a black or black-brown race, found originally in Africa, notable for thick lips, kinky hair', etc. Sometimes an entire entry with several meanings is badly managed. For example, take the adjective *Gothic*. Basically this means pertaining to the Goths, a Germanic people who in the fifth century sacked Rome and who because of their depredations came to be a type of barbarian and representative of the Dark Ages. So, in later times, the word was applied, originally unfavourably, to a medieval style of architecture now much admired, and to a rather fantastic type of fiction, often with a medieval setting. As a noun *Gothic* means the language of the Goths, black letter print (because of its early use in the fifteenth century), etc. The entry *Gothic* must make this cluster of associations clear. It will not do to give the meanings disjointedly and with never a link to the Goths.

In any case not a great deal of leeway in the words or sentence forms possible for expressing the same meaning exists; and differences between one definition and another for the same meaning may be more or less unimportant. Yet there are good definitions, exact, succinct, and poor ones, ambiguous, or perhaps wordy. Finally, an editor may consult predecessor dictionaries and may decide that the definition in one of them for the sense on which he is engaged is so good that he can do no better than paraphrase it.

How narrow is the range of possibilities in some instances may be illustrated by the word *Mulatto*; *O.E.D.* has 'One who is the offspring of a European and a Negro; also used loosely for any half-breed resembling a mulatto'. The relation of the *D.A.E.* definition to the *O.E.D.* is obvious: 'One who is the offspring of a Negro and a white person; a Negro with some white blood'. The reason for the difference in the second part is due to the fact that, since the quotations in *D.A.E.* are limited to American matter, there is no possible reference to the mixture of East

Indian and Negro blood which is mentioned in one of *O.E.D.*'s quotations. The *A.C.D.* has: 'The offspring of parents of whom one is white and the other a Negro'. *Merriam-Webster* makes an effort to avoid the familiar pattern with: 'The first generation offspring of a pure negro and a white; in popular use, any person of mixed Caucasian and negro blood'. No doubt this last is more precise than the other definitions; yet it may be questioned whether any ordinary reader would suppose that offspring meant second or third generation descendant. At any rate, obviously the range in words usable for this definition is limited, and many definitions allow hardly much more variation. This is particularly true of definitions of plants and animals. For example, *Pigeon hawk* is defined in *Merriam-Webster* as: 'Any of several small hawks; esp., a small American falcon (*falco columbarius*) related to the European merlin. The sharp-shinned hawk'. *D.A.E.* has: 'Any of several small hawks esp. the American merlin, *Falco columbarius*'. *The American College Dictionary* reads: 'A small American true falcon, *Falco columbarius*, closely related to the merlin'. It would not require remarkable ingenuity for a lexicographer to frame one of those definitions without any special knowledge of ornithology; I am sure that the *D.A.E.* definition was made by such an editor, who perhaps consulted *Birds of America*.

On the other hand, there are definitions which none but an expert in the subject which they concern should touch. When the *D.A.E.* approached the philosophical word *pragmatism*, I knew this was a case in point; so I asked a well-known philosopher to give us a definition for it. What he provided was a bit too long for the scale on which we were operating; we condensed it somewhat, and after consultation the definition as printed was agreed upon: 'An American philosophical movement founded by C. S. Peirce (1839–1914) and William James (1842–1910), characteristic doctrines of which are that the practical consequences of a conception are the expression of its whole meaning, and that the object of thinking is to develop general principles of conduct.' Examination of the definitions in the *Merriam-Webster* and *The American College Dictionary*, both no doubt made by philosophers, show very little similarity in phrasing. In keeping with its scale *Merriam-Webster* has more encyclopedic information, which I should think might be received gratefully by an unphilosophic reader.

There are many aspects of definition-making that might be discussed. For example, Johnson pointed out that in defining the simplest words it is impossible to avoid the use of more elaborate words. At times he met the situation by not attempting an exact definition, as in his well-known words for *Cat* – a familiar domestic animal. Actually the only features which distinguish that from a recent definition: 'a domesticated carnivore, *Felis domestica* (or *F. catus*), widely distributed in a number of breeds', are pretentious phrasing and the Latin terms. Without the latter the definition could be applied to a dog (in fact it *is* applied to a dog in that dictionary, with differences only in the Latin – *canis familiaris* – and the variation 'bred in a great many varieties'), and to the general reader the Latin means merely that presumably it is the zoological term for *cat*; so really he has got nothing from the definition. Hence Johnson was right both in his observation about the impossibility of defining the simplest words except by the use of more elaborate ones and in his decision to make no real effort to define *cat*.

On occasion, however, Johnson, perhaps carried away by his love of ornate diction and his pride in his mastery of it, contrived definitions so intricate as to arouse amusement even in his own day. A famous one is that for *Network*: 'any thing reticulated or decussated, at equal distances, with interstices between the intersections'. Admittedly *reticulate* as an adjective had been in use for a century before Johnson's use of it here; and so had *decussated*. But modern dictionaries have no difficulty in defining *network*. For example, the *O.E.D.* has: 'Work in which threads, wires, or similar materials, are arranged in the fashion of a net'. Rarely does one find anything approaching such Johnsonian definitions in books of recent date; but in *O.E.D.* I notice: 'Sand. A material consisting of comminuted fragments and water-worn particles of rocks (mainly silicious)'. In their definitions of the word neither *Merriam-Webster* nor *A.C.D.* find it necessary to use *comminuted* or *silicious*, both of which are meaningless to me, or to use any words which are not in ordinary speech or easily understood. Lexicographers have developed an art in defining which, aside from the need of using technical Latin names for plants, animals and other subjects like those studied in such sciences as anatomy and geology, is able to make clear the meaning of words without having to resort to erudite terms which have significance only for specialists.

Yet one can have such experiences as the following still: Trying to assemble a plastic model of a motor car for a little boy, I was following directions which recommended *balsa cement*. Curious as to what this might be, I looked up the term in two recent dictionaries; neither had it, but both define *balsa*. One definition started thus: 'a bombacaceous tree, *Ochroma lagopus*'. *Bombacaceous*, what a word! Looking that up, I read: 'belonging to the *Bombacaceæ*, a family of woody plants'. Possibly I had learned something, but it surely wasn't much.

One cannot leave Johnson without mention of a type of definition associated with his name: that in which he expressed a personal prejudice or a vagrant sense of fun. In proportion to the whole work there are very few of these, but some of them became so famous that they are always thought of as a feature of his dictionary. 'Lexicographer, a writer of dictionaries, a harmless drudge', is a humorous, deprecatory reference to himself. 'Excise, a hateful tax levied upon commodities, and adjudged not by the common judges of property, but by wretches hired by those to whom the Excise is paid' evidently reveals a personal detestation of that imposition. I know of only one dictionary which provides definitions of similar character; this is Ernest Weekley's *Etymological Dictionary*. The actually small number of slightly humorous or 'flip' definitions there were seized upon by reviewers with such delight that from their reports one might have supposed that the book was one of popular entertainment.

The problems of the commercial lexicographer at first sight seem simpler, but he has his troubles too. He need include only current words and senses and some obsolete words and meanings according to fixed principles, as we have seen on an earlier page, and he gives only an occasional quotation, or in the case of small books, none at all. If he is lazy or pushed for time, he may merely paraphrase the definitions available in another dictionary; but a conscientious dictionary-maker devotes the greatest care to the perfect expression of meanings and takes entirely proper pride in making sure that he has as many new words and meanings as possible – usually technical expressions coming from constantly expanding science and industry. For his definitions of such new terms he must rely chiefly on information supplied to him by experts and on the quotations which his readers have made; he can hardly know any of the new expressions from his own experience. Thus the latest *Merriam-Webster* has 105 senses for *set*, verb, because of the special technical uses in various industries. It must give the editor many a qualm to have to include so many senses which he must define on the word of others.

The commercial dictionary's solution of this problem is the engagement of specialists who supply such new technical words and meanings as they may have noticed and, perhaps more important, survey and correct the definitions, pronunciation, etc., of the words which are in their fields. How far back this practice goes I do not know, but as early as 1730 Nathaniel Bailey published a dictionary prepared with the help of two specialists. In his revision of his 1828 dictionary, Noah Webster had the assistance of a professor in a medical school who corrected and improved the definitions of the scientific words. This practice was followed in succeeding revisions of Webster's work, with ever-increasing numbers of experts. Similarly the other commercial dictionaries such as the *Standard*, the *Century* and the *American College* had staffs of consultants. The latest *Merriam-Webster* publishes portraits of 147 of these 'special editors'. This collaboration is managed in various ways in the preparation of new dictionaries or revisions of old ones. The method of the *Standard Dictionary* has been made clear in a book issued by its publisher: after the editorial staff had prepared their copy, it was set up and proofs were sent to the specialists. These made such corrections, additions and revisions of the information given for words in their fields as seemed to them desirable on the proofs and returned them to the editors, who incorporated the alterations in their copy for the press.

One might suppose that this checking of definitions and presumably rewriting of some, especially in a dictionary which has been revised, would result in such perfection that one could depend absolutely on the definitions provided. Unfortunately it does not work out so. The fault is not in the scholarship or scientific knowledge of the experts; they are often among the most eminent men in their respective fields. But it is true sometimes that notable scholars and experts in industry, politics, etc., have little sense of the way to express exact meaning and shades of meaning; the words are so familiar to them that in their own minds they supply the meaning without realising that the definitions before them do not adequately state their significance. In other words, they lack a *critical* sense as applied to definition. I have seen this lack even in a trained and experienced lexicographer, who did excellent editing, but when confronted with proofs of other men's editing, never questioned anything, much less detected any faults in definition. It requires a person of rather unusual intellectual qualities to make himself a master of some scientific study or a leader in politics or business and at the same time have a critical sense of the exact meaning of technical terms in his field, see faults in proposed definitions or definitions which have been in use, and, finally, have the ability to phrase definitions to replace them. Everyone has encountered specialists in science, industry, or some professional activity like social service, who have so little command of words that they cannot talk about their business without the use of technical jargon, and hence cannot make their ideas or experiences clear to a non-specialist. Such persons have no vocabulary with which to define technical expressions and so cannot perform lexicographical functions well.

Some time ago my daughter, then a student at college, wrote to me an inquiry as to the meaning of a philosophical word, one that is found frequently in books intended for the general public as well as in works of scholarship. This seemed to me an easy way in which to increase filial respect, for though I know no philosophy, I supposed that the dictionary on which I rely chiefly, one that has been revised many times, would have a perfect explanation of it. With considerable complacency, therefore, I copied the definition given there and sent it to her. Back came a sharp answer, stating that the definition was wholly inadequate and giving another which, I judge, she had got from her teacher. As far as I know, the teacher may have been wrong, but his definition had the appearance of being precise and thought out exactly. If so, the philosopher who examined the definitions for that dictionary had failed to realise that the definition did not express the meaning of the word distinctively. This is by no means the only instance of faults in definition in reputable dictionaries which have been pointed out to me or which I have observed myself.

No doubt the chief editor of a good commercial dictionary is well aware of the possibility of this sort of oversight in the scanning of definitions or of inept expression in the making of new definitions. No doubt he examines the work of his collaborators and weeds out those who, he perceives, are not dependable judges of definitions. At any rate, if dictionaries are to include technical words and meanings – as apparently they must, for otherwise how are you and I to find out what is the meaning of a technical expression that we encounter in our reading or in directions for assembling toys? – there seems to be no better way to secure accuracy and clarity than in the engagement of experts as co-labourers, and probably in a large proportion of words, the results of this method are satisfactory.

The lexicographer working at a historical dictionary has less difficulty of this sort than the commercial lexicographer, because his concern is only with the general stock of words which have been long in the language. A new word or meaning – and most technical terms are relatively new – has little or no history, and most such words do not turn up in the literature from which his quotations are taken. Consequently his own knowledge guided by the quotations in hand gives him a basis for judging the meanings of words and the right way to define them. Hence there is no corps of specialists attached to a historical dictionary, though of course the editor, especially if, as is generally the case, he is working in an academic environment, may ask colleagues for help in defining a term as used in special fields. In the main, however, the historical lexicographer relies on what he can

discern as to meaning in the quotations with which he is working, on glossaries to texts, on etymological meaning and on
earlier dictionaries. Perhaps the historical dictionary man may
rely too much on dictionary methods in making his definitions,
with the result that he does not realise that here or there a word
has a more specific sense than the one that he ascribes to it, on
the basis of his quotations and his understanding of the word's
general meaning. Thus it may be that an editor not steeped in
the philosophical writing of some early period may not realise
that an expression in a quotation from a philosophical text has
a more limited meaning than the one in ordinary use at the
time; at any rate, I have been told that some of the philosophical
terms in early English writings are not adequately defined in
The Oxford English Dictionary.

It is, however, only fair to the general lexicographer, whether
commercial or historical, to point out that his main function is
to explain the whole vocabulary of the language, and that if one
wants sure definitions of technical words and uses one should
consult a more specialised lexicon, e.g. of philosophy, social
sciences, medicine, etc. Heaven help the maker of a specialised
dictionary if his definitions are not accurate! It is his job to
make them so.

The dictionary-maker also must decide on how much information he will include in addition to the bare definition. Attention has been called to the fact that *The Century Dictionary* gives
encyclopedic explanation; but so to a less extent do all large
modern dictionaries. On account of their more limited space
smaller books must restrict themselves to mere definition. For
example, at *Lent*, the 1934 *Merriam-Webster* presents, in addition
to a definition, condensed statements about the history of the
observance of Lent since the fourth century, and the length of
the period in the Eastern and Western churches. *The American
College Dictionary*, on the other hand, gives only a definition.
Sometimes the information supplied is interesting, even novel,
e.g. this from *Merriam-Webster*: 'By act of July 24, 1897 . . . of
the Revised Statutes of the United States it is provided that all
rolls of tobacco, or any substitute therefor, wrapped with tobacco,
shall be classed as cigars, and all rolls of tobacco or substitute

therefor, wrapped in paper, or any substance other than tobacco, shall be classed as cigarettes.'

9. *Arrangement of senses*

Once the lexicographer has the senses of his word in mind, he is ready to arrange them. The historical lexicographer must arrange them in the chronological order of their development, as far as he can ascertain it; the commercial lexicographer can present them in any order that seems to him desirable, though in most cases he tries to put the original or basic meaning first. When, as in most cases, there are not more than four or five meanings, usually there is little difficulty in arranging them; but when there are multiple meanings it may require much cogitation to discern the true order of development. This is so in the making of a historical dictionary because it is not sufficient to place the senses in a simple series according to date of appearance.

Study of the proliferation of meanings, a study which was called *semantics* until that word was taken over by persons whose interest was limited to the social effects of words and their meanings, has shown that meanings spread out from a central significance, which may be preserved as in the case of *foot*, or may be known in earlier language but are no longer in use as in the case of *nice*, or may be entirely lost as in the case of *lord*. The process is one of transference, often by a kind of figure; but generally it proceeds repeatedly from the basic sense; thus from *foot* in its position at the bottom of the body, we get *foot* of a hill or a school class; from its function in walking we get *foot* as a verb which means to walk; from its size we get *foot* as a measure of length. Each of the derived meanings may become in turn a centre from which develop secondary meanings. Thus from the sense of *foot* as a measure, come 'the least distance or space', as in Shakespeare's 'I'll starve ere I rob a foot farther', and a special measure in tin mining. Such secondary meanings often develop late; hence if a simple chronological order were used their relation to the sense from which they came would not be shown. The process, which has been called *radiation*, is commonly represented by a scheme like this:

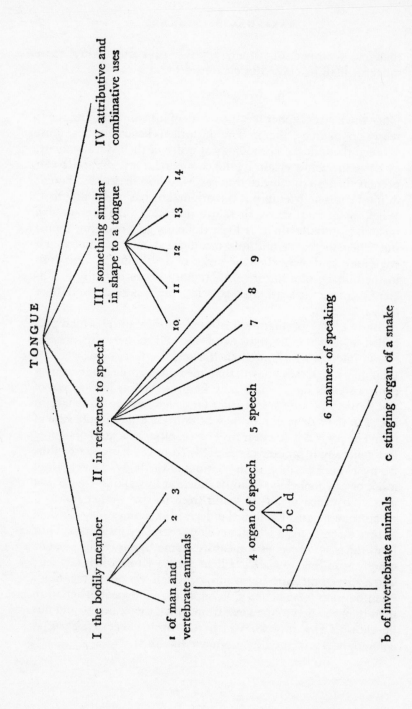

It is perhaps a pity that dictionary form does not permit the inclusion of diagrams like the one above, for they are instantly clear to the eye; in their place a system of numbering which can be overlooked easily or misunderstood is used. Murray's explanation of the system is so clear that it should be quoted:

Board names a material object; yet compare: a thin *board*, a frugal *board*, a card-*board*, *board* and lodgings, passengers on *board*, a *board* school, the *Board* of Trade, to tread the *boards*, a sea-*board* parish. The order in which these senses were developed is one of the most important facts in the history of the word; to discover and exhibit it are among the most difficult duties of a dictionary which aims at giving this history. If the historical record were complete, that is, if we possessed written examples of all the uses of each word from the beginning, the simple exhibition of these would display a rational or logical development. The historical record is not complete enough to do this, but it is usually sufficient to enable us to infer the actual order. In exhibiting this in the Dictionary, that sense is placed first which was actually the earliest in the language: the others follow in the order in which they appear to have arisen. As, however, the development often proceeded in *many* branching lines, sometimes parallel, often divergent, it is evident that it cannot be adequately represented in a single linear series. Hence, while the senses are numbered straight on 1, 2, 3, etc., they are also grouped under branches numbered I, II, III, etc., in each of which the historical order begins afresh. Sub-divisions of the senses, varieties of construction, etc., are marked a, b, c, etc.

When a word has but a few meanings, only the Arabic numbers are used. After a time it became customary for *O.E.D.*, in the case of words with many meanings, to give an outline or conspectus of the meanings before entering upon the detailed presentation of them.

How these principles and methods work out may be illus-trated by reference to the verb *set*. I. (The basic meaning) is 'to cause to sit, seat'. 1. 'To place in a sitting posture; to cause to occupy a seat; to seat', with a note: 'This sense is barely exem-plified outside certain phraseological expressions, e.g. to set on a seat', etc. The earliest quotation is dated about 888 and the latest 1735; this last indicates a fault in the material, for the usage is known to everyone as still current. There are three subordinate meanings attached to meaning 1: 'To cause (a body of persons) to sit in deliberation', marked obsolete, earliest quotation before 1122; 'To put (a hen) to sit on eggs', about 1440; 'To cause (a bird) to perch', 1530. Note that the arrangement of these subordinate meanings is that of the chronological order of the earliest quotations. Sense 2 is, 'To go down *upon one's knees*', about 1250. Sense 3 is the reflexive, 'to seat oneself, to take a seat, sit down', before 1300. Sense 4 is passive, 'To be seated', about 1330. Sense 4 has three sub-meanings, dated fourteenth century (certainly earlier than 1390), 1390, and 1801. Thus far the arrangement agrees with chronology as shown by earliest quotation; but 5 diverges, as its first quotation, about 1205, antedates 2, 3, and 4. This sense is defined as intransitive, 'To sit, be seated'. Here Henry Bradley (the editor of this section of *O.E.D.*) or the sub-editor who prepared this word, felt that since the verb basically has a transitive use, the transitive senses 2, 3, 4 must actually have come into use before the intransitive sense 4 did, even though this view was not supported by the evidence of the quotations. In other words this would be one of the occasions when in Murray's words 'the historical record is not complete enough'. In the *Dictionary of American English*, I think, we had to deviate from chronological order much more rarely than the *O.E.D.* because of the much briefer span of time which we were covering. Senses 6 and 7 follow. Then comes the second main meaning (II) with the definition 'to sink, descend', with sub-meanings 8, 9, etc.

A commercial dictionary, as has been said, need not follow the historical order. In the main *Merriam-Webster* does so with the omission of obsolete senses, which at times may obscure the fundamental arrangement, and the placing of all technical uses at the end of the entry. The *American College* makes this statement: 'The central meaning of each part of speech is put first; usually this is also the commonest meaning. The usual order after the central meaning is: figurative or transferred meanings, specialised meanings, obsolete, archaic, or rare meanings. This order, however, has been broken wherever it is desirable to group related meanings together and for other reasons.' In other words the commercial editor feels free to arrange meanings in the order which seems to him most desirable for the particular word on which he is engaged.

10. *Quotations*

A word or two concerning the choice of quotations. In selecting those to be used, the editor is guided by several considerations: he must include the earliest quotation that he has for each sense; in the case of obsolete words or meanings he must give the latest one that he has; he has some rule as to the number of quotations to be used per century (in the *Dictionary of American English* if the word was colourless, the name of a plant or animal known in England or of an ordinary occupation, we inserted two quotations for each meaning per century but used many more if the word was an Americanism or involved something important in American life or if the quotations we had were particularly interesting). The best quotations are those which define word or meaning, or have value as information, e.g. in the case of *D.A.E.* those which revealed something of importance concerning American social history. It is hard to reject a quotation which is humorous. At the time that material is being gathered for the dictionary, readers are instructed to look for such quotations. Consider the following examples from the *D.A.E.*:

Salt meadow: 1933 Catlin *Indians* I.219. We came in contact with an immense saline, or 'salt meadow', as they are termed in this country . . . some hundreds of acres of the prairie which were covered with an incrustation of salt.

Stalwart: 1881 *Nation* 16 June 415/2. The epithet 'Stalwart' . . . was first used by Mr Blaine in 1877 to designate those Republicans who were unwilling to give up distrust of the South as a political move.

Entertainment: 1898 Page *Red Rock* 156. Jacquelin's arrest and illness had come near breaking up the entertainment (a name which had been substituted for ball, to meet the scruples of . . . pious ladies).

Cherokee: c1849 Paige *Dow's Sermons* I. 155. There are all kinds of gibberish, from Cherokee up to Chaldee – but I consider the old English the best of any agoing.

In the article Dictionary in the *Encyclopædia Britannica*, which in

F

the main shows a fundamental comprehension of the aims and methods of lexicography, there are two remarks about the choice of quotations which I should decidedly question. The first of these runs as follows:

> A quotation which contains an important bit of historical evidence must be used, whether its source is 'good', from the literary point of view, or not – whether it is a classic of the language or from a daily newspaper; though where choice is possible, preference should, of course, be given to quotations extracted from the works of the best writers.

For the observation in the *though* clause I cannot see the slightest justification. The purpose of a historical dictionary is not to provide models of good writing, as was Johnson's aim and presumably that of Charles Richardson, whose dictionary was in that respect admirable. The purpose of showing the history of words quite overrides that of providing 'illustrative' quotations, which the *Encyclopædia* in its next sentence says is 'still recognised as highly important'. This, in my opinion, simply is not true; by the nature of its plan a historical dictionary could not possibly give more than a small number of quotations from classical authors; it cannot have the secondary function of providing models of good diction. The same misconception appears again in the article in the following sentence concerning *The Oxford English Dictionary*:

> A minor fault is that excerpts from second or third rate authors have occasionally been used where better ones from writers of the first class must have been at hand or could have been found.

The suggestion that an editor used a poor quotation from an obscure author in preference to a better one by anyone else is silly. Not for an instant does an editor forget that it is his job to use the best quotations. His proper procedure is, as he well knows, to select the best quotations correctly spaced in time, regardless of their source.

Commercial dictionaries, especially the large ones, use occasional quotations, but on no principle that I can discern. Presumably the purpose of the editors in including them is to illustrate proper usage; and for that purpose examples derived from eminent authors would seem desirable.

11. *'Restrictive labels'*

One further task of the editor, in the case of words not in present accepted use, is to characterise their usage, e.g. as *obsolete, slang, colloquial, dialectal*. The affixing of what one dictionary calls 'restrictive labels' is governed by nothing except the judgment of the editor and his advisers; there is no absolute criterion. Thus *Merriam-Webster* labels *movie* as *slang*, *A.C.D.* as *colloquial*; *A.C.D.* marks *jitter* as *slang*, but does not label *jitterbug* at all; *Merriam-Webster* characterises *dunk* as *originally dialect U.S.*; *A.C.D.* gives it no label.

It is true, of course, that the status of a word may change in no great time, so that the label may need to be changed. For example, I should not like to have to label certain senses of *graft*. These do not appear in *O.E.D.* probably because of the date of publication of the section containing that word (January, 1901). In the *Supplement*, however, they are given with the label, *U.S. slang*. The first of these senses, 'A means of making illicit profit,' starts with a quotation dated 1889. This entire sense is omitted from *D.A.E.* probably because *Merriam-Webster* marked this sense as *slang*, and the *D.A.E.* had a rule that slang words and meanings were not to be included unless there was evidence of them before 1875. Yet that rule was not always observed; there is in fact another sense of *graft*, 'a calling or employment' marked in *D.A.E. slang* but not starting until 1896, which is included – an oversight? Finally the sense 'illicit or dishonest gain usually secured through abuse of office', appears in *D.A.E.* unlabelled. (Remember that it is marked *slang* in the *O.E.D. Supplement*.) Similarly *grafter*, labelled *chiefly U.S. colloquial*, is in *D.A.E.* without label. Surely *O.E.D.* is inconsistent, for if these senses of *graft* are slang, *grafter* must be too. And of course *D.A.E.* is also. To my mind, that of an elderly American, affected no doubt by the conservatism of age, neither *graft* (in these senses) nor *grafter* is in entirely reputable use, though both words are indispensable. It is certainly true, however, that they are in much better use now than they were in (say) 1910.

12. *Reading the proofs*

Having completed his work on the meanings of words and on their usage, the historical lexicographer has finished his task, except for one laborious responsibility, the reading of the proofs not only of his own editing but also of that of his colleagues. Here a kind of critical sense which, as we have seen, is not possessed by every dictionary-maker, comes into play. The editor must scrutinise every feature of the work, and a critical mind will perceive ways of improving the text, especially that prepared by his colleagues! Most corrections and suggestions will be made on the first proofs, which are long 'galleys'. In former times, especially in England, it was possible for editors to rewrite the text on the galleys – a highly desirable condition for editors because when one sees the text in print one can see many ways of improving it. Nowadays on account of printing costs alterations even on the galleys must be limited severely, at least in the United States. On the page proofs the editor will aim chiefly to make sure that alterations and corrections marked on the galleys have been made and that no new errors in details such as spelling and punctuation have crept in.

13. *Non-lexicographical features*

Work on a commercial dictionary continues, however, whether it is to be done by the editor or by other members of the staff. It has long been the custom for such books to offer additional information more or less related to the dictionary proper. Thus Samuel Johnson provided an English grammar and a history of the English language; and Webster even in his first short dictionary (1806) included tables of money, weights and measures, statistics of population and a history of the world. Later, matter somewhat more germane to the nature of a dictionary was added frequently, especially dictionaries of proper names, geographical and personal. The 1934 *Merriam-Webster* has such supplements, a 'pronouncing gazetteer' and a 'biographical dictionary', a list of famous people with dates of birth and death and a phrase characterising them. Some dictionaries like the *Standard* and the *American College* incorporate personal and place-names and the names of famous people into the main vocabulary.

These are certainly not essential parts of a dictionary; they are not included in the *O.E.D.* or the *D.A.E.* Some who write about lexicographical theory object to their inclusion as they do to the use of pictures. Doubtless it is true that theoretically a dictionary should deal only with the ordinary words in the language and that proper names are outside its scope; and one can argue that it should be possible by purely linguistic means to define all words, i.e. that pictures ought not to be needed. But this kind of theory, it seems to me, if actually followed, would decrease the value of a general dictionary vastly. Certainly English historical dictionaries do not use pictures; but their purpose is to give historical information and to trace the growth of the vocabulary. Even so a former editor of the *Middle English Dictionary* told me that he planned to include encyclopedic material and pictures; such a book as he intended would have been not only an explanation of medieval English words but a digest of medieval English life and art. Surely the more a book gives the better. Theory that would exclude pertinent matter which increases the clarity of the whole treatment is sterile; and it is undeniably handy to be able to find information about places and persons of eminence in the same volume which contains explanation of the common words of the language.

As to pictures, it is so inane to point out that at a glance a picture makes many subjects, e.g. animals, plants, terms in architecture, clearer than many words can do, that I blush to do so. In identifying criminals Bertillon measurements are invaluable for confirmation of a suspicion, but for recognising a 'wanted' man there is nothing to compare with the pictures that are circularised. Ever since the publication of *The Century Dictionary* its use of pictures and the pictures themselves have been praised (it is said that Ernest Thompson Seton, a famous artist of the time, who devoted himself especially to animal drawings, made a thousand of them); and by permission they have been used by other dictionaries; the pictures in the recent *Dictionary of Americanisms* were prepared with great care and are helpful.

The tradition of prefixing to a dictionary a history of the English language and other treatises is maintained in some dictionaries. Thus the *Merriam-Webster* of 1934 has a history of the language and, even more notable, a treatise on phonetics by a recognised American authority, Professor John S. Kenyon; a study of this would help many who consult a dictionary to understand the pronunciation better than they can otherwise. *The American College Dictionary* has a 'Guide to Usage' that ought to be very useful to many students and the general public.

ENGLISH DICTIONARIES OF LIMITED SCOPE

An argument could be made for including given or 'Christian' names even in an historical dictionary. Certainly we need to know the history of Arthur, Henry, Albert, Mary, Edith, etc., in English. Some occur in Anglo-Saxon; more were introduced from French after the Norman Conquest; some are not found until comparatively late times; yet *The Oxford English Dictionary* does not include them. Fortunately one can find in most commercial dictionaries at least the derivation and original meaning of them. Evidently they must wait for a special dictionary, as must more properly surnames.

For the names of places in England, however, we have an admirable dictionary. Much attention has been devoted to place-names during the nineteenth and especially the twentieth centuries, and many monographs on the names found in various counties have appeared, giving etymologies and sometimes the history of the spelling of the place-names which occurred. The whole matter was placed on a scientific basis as a result of the founding of the English Place-Name Society; its first publication, a general introduction to the study of English place-names, appeared in 1924. The Society publishes in rapid succession a series of monographs on the names found in particular counties, all on essentially the same plan. The authors of these are scholars whose knowledge of method and of the language involved is exact and thorough. On the completion of several studies a dictionary incorporating the principles of these investigations was published under the editorship of Professor Eilert Ekwall (1877-1964), a distinguished Swedish scholar, who had worked for years on English place-names; its title is *The Concise Oxford Dictionary of English Place-Names*, 1936.

No similar study of American place-names has been made,

though attention has been devoted to the names which occur in a few states, and a good monograph has been published by Professor Robert L. Ramsay on the place-names of Missouri. Except for the Indian place-names in the United States, the information which systematic study would bring forth would lack much of the interest of place-names in England with their long history and derivation from such languages as early Irish and Welsh, popular Latin, Anglo-Saxon and Old Norse. Probably the fact that the material of an American place-name dictionary would consist so much of names borrowed from well-known foreign places like Waterloo and New York, compounded from the names of early settlers like Smithtown and Hessville, names of no importance at all, has deterred scholars from the labour of compilation.

Another dictionary important for the study of English is Joseph Wright's *English Dialect Dictionary*. This has a history much like that of the place-name dictionary, but it far antedates the latter. Just as monographs on the place-names of several counties had to be made before there could be a dictionary of place-names, and as the Early English Text Society had to publish many Middle English texts in order to lay a basis for the treatment of Middle English in *The Oxford English Dictionary*, so before a dialect dictionary could be made, thorough study of the several dialects had to be completed. There had been much disconnected study of English dialects since the seventeenth century, and one famous work had been published: Jamieson's *Etymological Dictionary of the Scottish Language*, in 1808–25. But more systematic and comprehensive surveys were needed. So W. W. Skeat, long professor at Cambridge, author of the *Etymological Dictionary* and editor of many early texts, founded the English Dialect Society in 1873. By the time that the Society was discontinued in 1896, it had issued eighty publications, mostly monographs on different dialects. In addition, Skeat had gathered some materials in manuscript.

The task of making a dictionary from this mass of data was entrusted to a remarkable man, Joseph Wright, professor of comparative philology at Oxford. As a boy he was put to work in mills for a wage of a few pence a day. Quite illiterate, he taught himself to read and write in order to be able to read, as his fellow workers were doing, the news of the Franco-Prussian War. Later he regarded his early illiteracy as an asset in his study of dialects. In the preface to his *English Dialect Grammar*, originally published in the final volume of his *Dictionary*, he wrote:

> As I did not learn to read until I was practically grown up, the knowledge of my own dialect – uninfluenced by the literary language – has been of considerable use in the writing of this grammar, and has enabled me to avoid mistakes which would certainly have been made by anyone who had not spoken a dialect pure and simple in his youth.

Moreover, by speaking in dialect himself he could get those from whom he was seeking information to use and explain their dialects unaffectedly.

Though handicapped by poverty, Wright managed to get to Germany and there to obtain a doctor's degree. Returned to England, he succeeded Max Müller at Oxford, married one of his pupils (who became co-author with him of many grammars of medieval languages, books unusually well adapted to the needs of students, and alone contributed valuable articles to philological journals), and after supplementing the materials gathered by the Dialect Society with data obtained by his own inquiries, published, it is said at his own expense, the *English Dialect Dictionary* (1896–1905).

This book is beyond all praise; it provides more detailed information than, I should suppose, anyone could have anticipated before the work actually appeared. In 1905 Wright wrote: 'The writing of this grammar was begun none too soon, for had it been delayed another twenty years I believe it would by then be quite impossible to get together sufficient pure dialect material,' because the use of dialect in England was disappearing. Obviously the *Dictionary* also could not have been produced had not the materials been collected before the first World War.

No similar dictionary of American dialects exists, primarily because no proper foundation has been laid for one. Of course there has been an American Dialect Society for many years;

but its publications have been limited to random word lists for various localities, and notes about individual dialect expressions, set forth in its periodical *Dialect Notes*. Far more systematic surveys of the peculiarities of local speech would have to be made before a dictionary comparable with Wright's could be compiled. Nevertheless, a few years ago Professor Harold Wentworth published *A Dictionary of American Dialects* on the basis of the material in the possession of the American Dialect Society, random articles in print here and there and his own collections. This is necessarily incomplete, but it makes available a good deal of interesting information as to expressions in popular use.

It should be realised, of course, that even a relatively complete dictionary of American dialects would not have the same interest or significance as the *English Dialect Dictionary*. For one thing, dialects in the United States are by no means so pronounced as were those in England in the nineteenth century and earlier. English travellers have remarked repeatedly on the uniformity of speech in the United States; anything approaching the condition in England can be found only in a few districts cut off by geographical barriers from the ordinary life of the nation. Moreover, American dialects do not have the historical significance that English dialects have as confirming our knowledge of dialect boundaries in Middle English, of the meaning of some Middle English words which have been lost in standard English, and of the history of sounds and forms.

DICTIONARIES OF SLANG

One final type of English dictionary, that dealing with slang, must be mentioned. In many treatments of this element in English, it should be noted, slang is associated with cant, the lingo of criminals and vagabonds, which has a purpose quite different from that of what is now ordinarily meant by slang, namely, to enable its speakers to communicate with each other in the presence of law-abiding persons without being understood by the latter. Cant, also, is a sort of technical speech; indeed, Greenough and Kittredge make a clean-cut distinction between slang and cant by associating cant with the technical vocabularies of trades, arts and sciences, which are now called jargon.

How much secrecy can be preserved by the use of cant must be
problematical; one would suppose that the police and judges in
the criminal courts would learn the meanings of cant expressions not long after they come into use. However that may be,
certainly slang is not nowadays connected in our minds with
thieves' jargon. Yet as late as 1910, the article on slang in the
Encyclopædia Britannica by Henry Bradley still blends the two;
and the ancestors of modern slang dictionaries were dictionaries
of cant, which insensibly increased their range to include slang.
It may be of interest to note that the first meaning of *slang* in
Merriam-Webster is 'cant of thieves, beggars, gypsies, etc.', and
it is not labelled 'historical'. The dominant meaning of *slang*
now, however, is the body of new expressions (whether new
words like *jitney* and *jalopy*, or new meanings of words in accepted
usage like *joint* meaning place of resort or dwelling-place)
widely used in informal speech, usually for vigorous or humorous
effect. Some slang is old, e.g. *booze*, which in such spellings as
bouse, bowze goes back at least to the sixteenth century, and *bit*,
usually in such expressions as *two bits*, twenty-five cents, and
four bits, fifty cents, which is certainly more than a hundred
years old; but most of it is so recent that the more sedate members of society may never have heard it.

American slang, of course, differs from English slang; as used
in the movies (English *cinema*) and contemporary fiction,
American slang arouses the astonishment of English folk. Many
Americans are proud of their slang, regarding it as especially
expressive and 'unique'; some think that only the United States
has slang. The truth is that American slang, in keeping with
that boastfulness and forthputtingness which was offensive to
such British observers as Dickens and Mrs Trollope, is more
assertive, more dynamic than English slang, which to a large
extent relies on that negative understatement or litotes which
has been a characteristic of English speech from Anglo-Saxon
times on. Certainly there is plenty of English slang; in reading
English light fiction I encounter many words which are strange
and meaningless to me.

As we have noted, modern English slang dictionaries developed out of dictionaries of cant, which, as brief alphabetical

word lists, began to appear in the sixteenth century. In the customary way of dictionaries, these became longer and longer, and in time began to include colloquial expressions used by the general population. By the eighteenth century works of note such as Captain Grose's *Classical Dictionary of the Vulgar Tongue*, 1785, made their appearance and ran through several editions. In the nineteenth century the dictionary of J. C. Hotten was published and republished; and the larger work of Barrère and Leland in two volumes appeared. Finally in 1890–1904 came the most pretentious work of this sort, the dictionary of John S. Farmer, noted for his reprints of early English dramas, and W. E. Henley, the famous poet and editor. This book, which was published in abridged forms also, attempted to present slang historically and comparatively, by means of definition and quotations, from newspapers, and books which, chiefly in dialogue, use informal speech, e.g. Dickens's novels. For comparisons it drew upon French and German slang. As it is of the nature of slang to be evanescent, old expressions falling out of use and new ones being added constantly, adequate lexicographical treatment of it would require either new dictionaries at frequent intervals or completely new editions of a standard one at short intervals of time. In fact, in 1909 a book intended as a supplement to Farmer and Henley was published, but since then nothing has been done to modernise that book. Instead a new historical dictionary by Eric Partridge has been published and has run into five editions. This is a husky volume of 1,230 double-columned pages. Like Farmer and Henley, it necessarily relies chiefly on printed sources; it is a mine of information.

Three dictionaries and one large thesaurus of American slang have appeared. The earliest, by James Maitland, a newspaper man, came out in 1891. This modest effort included also English slang. A more ambitious work, by M. H. Weseen, appeared in 1934. Though this is a dictionary, it is arranged by topics, perhaps because of realisation that slang differs in the classes who use it; thus there are such topics as: Crooks and Criminals, Hoboes and Tramps, Railroaders, Loggers and Miners, and finally general slang (122 pages). There is an index by words of 100 pages; this is important since it enables one readily to find a given word under whatever topic it may be placed. The whole work comprises 543 pages. There are no quotations and merely brief definitions. A yet more comprehensive dictionary of American slang, containing 687 pages, was published in 1960 by Stuart Berg Flexner, who worked in close collaboration with Professor Harold Wentworth, the well-known dialectologist already mentioned.

The thesaurus by L. V. Berrey and M. van den Bark, 1942, was reprinted five times by 1947; and a second edition appeared in 1952. In order to make clear what a prodigious work this is, perhaps I should explain what is meant by *thesaurus*, especially since three dictionaries which I have consulted make no distinction between *thesaurus* and *dictionary*. It is true that 'thesaurus' has been applied to dictionaries of the classics. But in English and American usage the word (which means 'treasury' in Latin) names a book of synonyms and perhaps antonyms, the purpose being to assist in 'vocabulary building', i.e. extending the range of words which a person uses, and specifically to enable writers to avoid over-use of particular words and perhaps to express themselves with exact shades of meaning, since few synonyms are completely identical in meaning, and so a writer may find in the list of synonyms a word that states his meaning more precisely than the one with which he started. Probably the limitation of *thesaurus* to mean a book of this sort is due to *Roget's Thesaurus*, which has been enormously popular, having appeared in countless reprints and new editions since its first appearance in 1852.

A thesaurus of slang is essentially a bilingual book, as the entries are ordinary English words and the synonyms are slang. A small book of this sort (120 pages) by Howard N. Rose, 1934, explains in some introductory words that it will be useful to writers who wish to use slang in fiction. What other use there can be for a thesaurus of slang I can't imagine. But it seems rather a feeble reason for putting such an immense body of materials as Berrey and van den Bark had into the form of a thesaurus. Perhaps the reason that these editors chose the thesaurus plan is that it enabled them to get into print an amount of matter which in dictionary form would have required several volumes and would have taken many years to prepare, for a thesaurus does not give definitions (these compilers, however, do explain locutions when they see possibilities of obscurity of meaning), or pronunciations or etymologies (there is a small section offering suggestions as to derivation of a limited number of words).

The first edition of Berrey and van den Bark's book contained 842 pages and an index of 332 pages; the second edition expands this to 903 pages of text and 369 pages of index. The arrangement is by topics such as General Relations, Time, Order, Change, Resemblance, etc., and by trades. The editors must have had many informants, as the body of slang words is huge, and they have the appearance of being mostly words derived from speech, not writing. By means of the index it ought to be possible to find the meaning of almost any slang word in which one is interested; but one will get no further information as one would in a dictionary.

A retired college professor is of all men the least equipped to judge books on slang, because as a rule such a person's whole life is spent in an environment in which slang is rarely used. So I can form only an amateur's opinion of the completeness, the validity of the definitions or the currency of the vocabulary in the dictionaries of slang. Farmer and Henley certainly include much obsolete slang, and so, no doubt, do the others. Any book dealing with slang that derives part of its material from other books, except perhaps those published within the preceding three or four years, must contain much that is no longer current. Berrey and van den Bark's *Thesaurus*, however, has the appearance of being based on actual oral usage and containing the great mass of American slang expressions.

The fascination that cant or thieves' jargon exercises on men's minds has resulted in the publication of three notable dictionaries. The first of these, which appeared in 1931, was *American Tramp and Underworld Slang*, by Godfrey Irwin. The author states that his material was derived from twenty years' experience as a tramp – a scholarly tramp, as his careful collection of words and his exact definitions show. The volume contains an essay by Eric Partridge, who points out the origin of many American cant expressions in earlier colloquial English.

In 1950 appeared a remarkable book, which deals not with slang but with thieves' jargon. The material for the *Dictionary of American Underworld Lingo*, edited by Goldin, O'Leary and Lipsius, was assembled not from printed sources but from the speakers themselves, who (it is said) included carnival workers, confidence men, burglars and hoboes. That men in and out of penitentiaries should care enough about their cant language to report upon cant vocabulary and assist in the compilation of a dictionary of it is astonishing. The work, a book of 327 pages, is in two sections both alphabetised; the first is arranged according to the cant words; the second is by English words, giving their cant equivalents. Model sentences are given to illustrate the meaning and idiomatic use of the cant words. To my eyes the book has the air of veracity, but of course I am even less competent to judge it than I am books on slang.

To many readers and scholars the most interesting of these books is Eric Partridge's *A Dictionary of the Underworld, British and American* (New York and London, 1950), because it gives an immense amount of information on the derivation and history of the words. Its method is that of the *Oxford Dictionary*; it is based on historical principles, with dated quotations arranged in chronological order; these extend in date from the sixteenth century to the present time. The work comprises 804 double-column quarto pages; as the accomplishment of one man working but a few years, it is phenomenal. Its revelation of the criminal mind and modes of living make it enormously interesting; indeed the Boston Public Library has to keep its copy in a locked case to prevent its being stolen.

THE USE OF A DICTIONARY

Most dictionaries, in a preliminary section, give directions and suggestions for the use of their text. This section includes explanation of the abbreviations used, of the method of showing pronunciation, indication of the kinds of information that may be found in the word entries, what is meant when, in the etymology, the source of the word is shown by an abbreviation but the original word is not actually printed, etc. Needless to say, it behoves one who wishes to get all that the book offers on the word one is looking up to give the time necessary to fix in mind what the abbreviations, the diacritical marks used in indicating pronunciation, etc., mean.

Under the influence of old tradition as well as conceptions of grammar, some dictionaries make separate entries for each part of speech, when a word is used as more than one part, thus gauge, *n.*, gauge, *v.*; rifle, *n.*, rifle, *v.*; good, *adj.*, goods, *n.* Others have but one entry, under which they arrange the meanings in blocks according to parts of speech. To a person with old-fashioned education the former method may seem the only natural one, for we were trained to regard the parts of speech as occupying separate, watertight compartments. But it must be admitted that in a language in which any noun may be used as a verb, if a verbal sense is required, or as an adjective, without addition of prefix or suffix, e.g. *ship* as noun or verb or adjective (of course one can wriggle out of the last by calling it an attributive use of the noun – but to what good?), it may be that the parts of speech in English have not enough reality to be worth emphasis, and perhaps the distinction should be given up altogether as it is in Jespersen's school grammar.

Commercial dictionaries generally give a type of information not to be found in historical dictionaries, but of potential value to anyone who is composing an article or speech: they list synonyms and antonyms, words of sense opposed to the word under consideration. In this connection, sometimes the dictionary makes helpful distinctions in sense among the synonyms, for there are relatively few absolute synonyms in English; in most cases there are differences of usage or shades of meaning.

From the quotations in a historical dictionary, one can usually perceive what is the idiomatic use of words, the prepositions which follow it, etc.; but a commercial dictionary, if it is a good one, makes explicit effort to state what one needs to know about the idiomatic usages; for example, it comments on whether different *to* or different *from* is correct, makes clear that compensation *for*, revel *in*, foist *on* or *upon*, etc., are in the best use.

Moreover, a good commercial dictionary often lists idiomatic phrases in which the word figures – information that may be deduced from the entry and quotations in a historical dictionary, or may not, but is given systematically in the commercial work.

HOW TO READ ETYMOLOGIES

Dictionaries vary greatly in the amount of detail given in their etymological information. The smaller books restrict themselves to the bare citation of the source and perhaps a cognate or two; the *Oxford Dictionary* and *Merriam-Webster* allow more space and cite many more allied words. For the non-specialist in language, actually the briefer treatment is clearer, less subject to misunderstanding. Thus if on looking up *brother*, one finds Anglo-Saxon *brōthor* and possibly a cognate like German *Bruder*, one is not likely to become confused. But when one finds after Anglo-Saxon *brōthor*, Latin, Greek, Lithuanian and Sanskrit words cited, one may reach wrong conclusions. To be sure, the dictionary probably has given the facts quite accurately, thus fr(om) A.S. *brōthor*, akin to (words perhaps in ten languages). This means that the word is derived from A.S. but that the A.S. word goes back ultimately to the same remoter source as the Greek, Latin, Sanskrit and other words cited; but I have known intelligent college students who from such entries supposed that the word was derived from Sanskrit. Perhaps what the dictionary means in such a case can be made clear by the genealogical scheme on p. 97.

Unfortunately some dictionaries complicate matters and mislead those who consult them for etymologies by citing the Middle English form as the first item in the etymology. Yet there is no etymological significance in the M.E. form, and no more point in giving it than there would be in citing a sixteenth-century spelling of the word. The real source of the word is the *next* item after the M.E. spelling. In a few instances, e.g. *boy*, *girl*, dictionaries can give nothing beyond the M.E. word except allied words in other languages, because the word is not found in Anglo-Saxon or any language from which it can have been derived. In other words, the etymology is unknown.

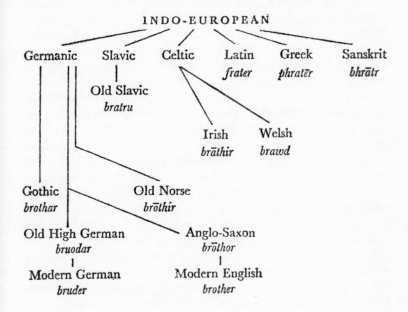

INDO-EUROPEAN

Germanic   Slavic   Celtic   Latin   Greek   Sanskrit
                                       frater   *phratēr*   *bhrātr*

Old Slavic
bratru

Irish   Welsh
brāthir   *brawd*

Gothic   Old Norse
brothar   *brōthir*

Old High German   Anglo-Saxon
bruodar   *brōthor*

Modern German   Modern English
bruder   *brother*

THE SIGNIFICANCE OF THE FIRST QUOTATION IN A
HISTORICAL DICTIONARY

In the compilation of a historical dictionary, as we have noticed, great effort is devoted to the attempt to get the earliest possible dated quotation for each word and each meaning of a word. But in only a few instances can it be hoped that the first quotation is within fifty years or so of the date of the first oral use of the word. Those few instances are generally words that are in some way or other topical; e.g. *bowdlerize* is derived from the name of T. Bowdler, who in 1818 published an expurgated edition of Shakespeare. *The Oxford English Dictionary*'s first quotation is 1836. *Icarian*, an early type of communist, is derived from the name of an imaginary republic in a book published in 1840. The *Dictionary of American English* has a quotation of 1851 in a French passage and one of 1867 in English, both meaning a member of a certain communist group in the United States.

Except for such rare instances, a historical dictionary can give no sort of guarantee that its earliest quotation for word or meaning is actually at all near to the earliest use in speech. Probably every student who has worked carefully over an early text has found in it earlier evidence for some words than the earliest citations in *The Oxford English Dictionary*. His study may show him that *O.E.D.* has quotations from his text, perhaps sufficiently numerous to make it clear that the text was read carefully for the *Dictionary*. Nevertheless, the reader overlooked some important words. As far as I can see there is no sure way of avoiding such oversight, no way by which the reader for a dictionary can surmise that this word or that in his text may be a first occurrence. The only way by which a lexicographer can be certain that he has all that a particular text has of value for his purpose is to have in his slips a complete concordance of the text. The *Middle English Dictionary* is using such concordances for texts which are regarded as of key importance; but obviously it would not be feasible to make concordances of many texts. Thus it is not correct to say that *The Oxford English Dictionary* shows that a word first appeared in English at a particular date or that the editors of *The Oxford English Dictionary* state that the word first appeared at such and such a date. A lexicographer is too conscious of the incompleteness of his material; all that the editors of *O.E.D.* say is that the earliest evidence that was available to them was of the date of their earliest quotation. A sizeable bibliography of notes and longer articles providing earlier quotations than the first in *O.E.D.* could be compiled. I myself contributed an article giving quotations from thirteenth- and fourteenth-century manorial documents of earlier date than *O.E.D.*'s.

THE AUTHORITY OF THE DICTIONARY

Often when people consult a dictionary they do so in order to learn the meaning of a word that is strange to them; but quite as often their motive is to find out what is correct in spelling, pronunciation, usage (colloquial, technical, slang, etc.), or meaning. With a childlike confidence they consult the dictionary confident that they will learn there what is correct; but ironically the makers of modern dictionaries explicitly disclaim the ability to state what is correct in hosts of matters under dispute where usage differs. They recognise the fact that to a large extent usage is not fixed. In fact in many instances there is no positive standard of what is correct; this is especially true as to pronunciation, less often as to meaning and usage (colloquial, slang, etc.). The 1934 *Merriam-Webster* has a series of quotations from specialists in English who make this point (p. xxvi).

A great change in attitude among those interested in the use of English has come about since the eighteenth century. At that time writers as well as the public in general believed that correctness was a reality, something that could be attained, and that it was important to obtain it. The purpose of the dictionary-maker then was to present what was correct in the spelling, meaning, and use of words, actually to omit anything that was 'low', and, from the time the dictionaries of Sheridan and Walker appeared, to set a standard of elegance and excellence in pronunciation. By the time Johnson wrote his preface, his experience as a lexicographer had made him realise that there is flexibility in usage, that language does not stay put but changes and grows. Still, in his dictionary his purpose was to 'ascertain' and fix usage. That attitude and aim have appeared in books down to the present day. The fact that not usage but some theoretical standard of correctness decides issues is apparent constantly in such a book as the Fowlers' *King's English*; the authors have a method of proceeding thus: first a rule, then a series of quotations, sometimes in two blocks, one marked 'right' the other marked 'wrong'. Opening the book at random (my copy is the second edition, 1908), I find on page 153 under 'wrong', H. Sweet (the great historical grammarian), Gladstone, Wilde (Oscar of course), Stevenson, and *The Times*. Similarly in H. W. Fowler's *Dictionary of Modern English Usage* under *shall* we find, 'The object will be to make the dry bones [of the rules for the use of *shall* and *will*] live by exhibiting sentences, all from newspapers of the better sort, in which one or other principle of idiom has been outraged'. Evidently the practice of authors of high standing and of newspapers of the better sort does not affect the standard of usage. No wonder that people feel that the rules of grammar are something recondite and ununderstandable. There are rebels, of course, against such hide-bound conceptions of grammar, who do not merely pay lip-service to the old criterion that present, reputable usage is acceptable but actually apply it. P. G. Perrin and Eric Partridge, in their dictionaries of usage, are less academic than were the Fowler brothers working together or H. W. Fowler alone.

All that may seem a digression as we are dealing not with grammar but with the dictionary. In my mind, however, it is not. What I am trying to get at is that throughout our school life and to some extent afterwards, we are so constantly being impressed with the idea of correctness, primarily in spelling (for the irregularities of spelling compel everyone to work at that intensely and for a long time), but also in grammar and pronunciation, that we are likely to feel that all aspects of English are hedged about with rules of right and wrong. In lexicography, however, ideas have changed, as they are beginning to do in grammar. No reputable dictionary now attempts to force people to pronounce *glass* with a different vowel sound from

that in *hat*. The attitude of lexicographers is that if in the com-
munity in which a person resides the prevailing pronunciation
of *path* has the same vowel sound as that in *rat*, people should
pronounce the word so. It is correct for me as a mid-Western
American to sound the *r* in *hard*, and for a Virginian to omit it.
Even in individual words recognition of previously unaccepted
pronunciation is made. For example, in my youth the pronunciation of *calliope* (a steam organ in a circus) in my com-
munity, and I suspect widely in the mid-West, had stress on the
first syllable and did not sound the final *e*; my pronunciation
was corrected so as to make it stress the second syllable and
sound the final *e* because that is the correct pronunciation of the
name of one of the Greek muses. Now I note that in a recent
dictionary, my old pronunciation is recognised as an alternate
to the other one. The modern dictionary attempts to assemble
and weigh all available evidence on a linguistic problem; it
does not merely follow tradition or give a single solution if usage
sanctions more than one. It does not hold that there is only one
correct use for Londoner, New Zealander, and Canadian, or
that it is possible or even desirable that all speakers of English
should speak or write alike. In the Introduction to *The American
College Dictionary*, Mr Barnhart epitomises the dictionary-maker's
attitude well: 'No dictionary founded on the methods of modern
scholarship can prescribe as to usage; it can only inform on the
basis of the facts of usage. . . . It is not the function of the
dictionary-maker to tell you how to speak, any more than it is
the function of the map-maker to move rivers or rearrange
mountains or fill in lakes.'

THE CHOICE OF A DICTIONARY

At first thought it might seem that the best dictionary to own
and use would be the *Oxford*, the 'unabridged' *Merriam-
Webster*, or the complete *Standard*, but this is not the case.
Oxford, for ordinary use, has several disadvantages: its ten
volumes make it very cumbersome to handle; it is not up-to-
date; none of it is more recent than the year 1933 and some of
it goes back as far as the late 1880s; but most important, the
great mass of its contents is of value only to specialists in

language or literature – the learned etymologies, the hosts of quotations, the details about the history of spelling, and the full treatment of obsolete words. Similarly, the 'unabridged' dictionaries contain much more than the average layman needs and are so large that they require a special stand or table for storage; in addition, usually they are not so up-to-date as smaller dictionaries. For ordinary purposes of showing spelling, pronunciation, meanings, and level of usage, the best books are the desk or 'college' dictionaries, particularly those which have been completely re-edited at least once (because in re-editing faults can be corrected and marked improvements made in the light of experience). An Englishman naturally should use a dictionary compiled in England as that will reflect British usage; and for similar reason an American should use a dictionary made in the United States. *The Concise Oxford Dictionary* would be best for literary and *Chambers's Twentieth Century* for general British use, though in the latter respect D. C. Browning's *Everyman's*, rather smaller, is very good; or, much larger than any of those three, H. C. Wyld's *Universal Dictionary*, whether for literary or for general use. The *Merriam-Webster Collegiate Dictionary*, one of the abridgements of the *Standard Dictionary*, the *American College*, or *Winston's* would be suitable for American use. I myself prefer the *Merriam-Webster*, but no doubt the others have advantages which make them superior for certain purposes.

RECENT ACHIEVEMENTS

Eric Partridge's *Origins, A Short Etymological Dictionary of Modern English* appeared in 1958, and its fourth revised edition in 1966. This author's other special dictionaries have already been described: *A Dictionary of Slang and Unconventional English* (p. 91) and *A Dictionary of the Underworld, British and American* (p. 94). In *Origins* Partridge treats the history of words in a most attractive and instructive way, leading the reader on from point to point pleasantly and helpfully. Instead of treating words separately, he links related forms together by means of an ingenious system of abbreviations and cross-references. For instance, he demonstrates clearly and completely the precise relationships between the adjective *sweet*, the verb *persuade*, the abstract noun *hedonism*, and all their cognates. The reader will find most of this information, it is true, in any reputable dictionary or glossary of etymology, but from Partridge's book he will gain a clearer and more detailed picture of the wide range of word-forms concerned. After a time he will catch something of Partridge's own enthusiasm for words and he will see the history of language in a new light.

In 1961 appeared the Third Merriam-Webster or, to give this work its full title, *Webster's Third New International Dictionary of the English Language Unabridged*. In fact, however, it is the eighth in that series of dictionaries which began with Noah Webster's famous one-man volume of 1828 (p. 26). Even more than its predecessors, this latest Webster is scientific and encyclopedic. It is indeed an entirely new compilation made by a team of specialists under the general editorship of Dr Philip Babcock Gove. Its etymologies have been constructed by Dr Charles Sleeth of Princeton. Sleeth made the very best use of the *Oxford* dictionaries and of all other available sources, but he encountered unforeseen difficulties when he came to write the word-histories of many thousands of neo-Hellenic scientific terms. As a practical and sensible solution to this problem he therefore decided to label their components ISV, thus denoting that they belong to a new International Scientific Vocabulary 'current in at least one language other than English'.

The Third Webster is both the most up-to-date and the most encyclopedic dictionary of the English language. Its 450,000 entries include numerous neologisms whose contextual meanings are illustrated by well-chosen citations from contemporary literature. It provides an authentic source for all those one-volume desk dictionaries, both American and British, which require constant revision in order to keep abreast of the most recent advances in science and technology.

The Third Webster came out just in time to be of service to E. McIntosh in his preparation of the fifth completely revised edition of *The Concise Oxford Dictionary of Current English*, which was published in 1964. Among English dictionaries this book now holds a place of exceptional importance since no revision of the *Shorter Oxford* has been undertaken since 1944 and no addition has been made to the great *Oxford Dictionary* itself after the *First Supplement* of 1933. Parts of the *Second Supplement*, long overdue, are at press and the completed volume or volumes will appear in 1970.

The year 1966 saw the publication of the long awaited *Oxford Dictionary of English Etymology* by Charles Talbut Onions, last surviving editor of *The Oxford English Dictionary* (1884–1928). Dr Onions died in January 1965 at the age of ninety-one and the *O.D.E.E.* was nothing less than his life-work. It contains nearly forty thousand entries and it holds a unique position as the highest authority on word-history throughout the whole English-speaking world.

INDEX

INDEX